EAST INDIA
Publishing Company

CONFESSIONS of a
MIDDLE-AGED WHITE MAN
John Wiber

Published by the
EAST INDIA PUBLISHING COMPANY
Ottawa, Canada

© 2022 East India Publishing Company

Cover Design by EIPC © 2022
9781774268087

www.eastindiapublishing.com

For Cathy

Contents

Intro

My mouth tastes of metal. Yellow patches stain the white ceiling like piss in snow. I can feel the broken bones in my nose rattling around as I attempt to draw air. My fucking jaw is broken...

I saw a dead crow on the ground this morning, lying on its back with its tiny black legs sticking rigidly in the air like abandoned flag poles, and black eyes that didn't blink. I remember at the time, I wondered if this dead bird was some sort of bad omen, a warning of some kind. But the idea was quickly disregarded, set aside in my realization that there was one and simple reason why that crow had died: humans. Whether it choked on our poisoned air or flew headfirst into a building, it was our fault the bird was dead. And there was really no other significance to it than that simple fact.

Messenger of death.

I can feel blood seeping through the back of my shirt, all warm and damp. Lying here sprawled out on the floor, a ringing in my head like sirens - too late - and while there are certainly more pressing matters that must be attended to, I cannot take my mind from my family, their faces flashing behind my eyes like a fast paced slideshow, and I wonder if I will ever get the chance to see them again, to say those things I want to say... so you can say sorry.

I can hear the rattling rasp of my companion who is lying somewhere behind me, but I cannot bear to turn around for the pain in my jaw and head is too great. I can feel my heart pulsating against my temple.

So, this is what it's come to?

My life.

1

So many spoiled days and wasted nights.

So many roads left untraveled. And so many responsibilities shelved in the wake of self-remorse and pettiness. My failure as a husband and father is epitomized in this warm pool of blood.

All these nagging regrets, like a house of cards, have come crashing down upon me.

Images of my wife and son flash behind my eyes. Blurred. Mere splotches inside my mind. And for the third or fourth time this week, my eyes well with tears, streaming down my face, mixing with all the blood and spit and snot, not because of the physical pain, but because of this writhing worm of guilt swimming in my gut. The bloody tears of a deranged and lonely man; a man who missed his family.

And as I lay here all bloodied and bruised, sobbing and laughing at the same time as ominous sentiments of sanity flitter through my mind, I think about how easy it is to take this life for granted, and how desperately afraid of death I truly am.

As the darkness descends over my eyes, I see her face, smiling back at me, and for some reason this fills me with a cold sort of calm, my chest slowly rising and falling like the gentle ebb and flow of the sea on a windless day, and I hope I can meet her, beyond this life, but then again, I highly doubt it, all things considered, because I am certain beyond a shadow of a doubt that if there is indeed an afterlife, I will reside in the darkest and deepest corners of Hell. Writhing and screaming as the flames lick my flesh, because I have not lived as I should, and I will burn until all that remains are hollow bones left to rot in an apathetic corner.

Sleep now.

Eternal Slumber come and rescue me from this life. Ah no, but that would be too easy, and somehow, I just know that I will survive. No matter how much I may want to die, I will go on living, like Cybil in the hourglass; I will grow envious of the dead and mourn my own existence.

And my mind crumbles in the wake of these realizations, my identity dissolving in a pit of acidic consciousness. I am a coward. I do not deserve your sympathy. There shall be no mercy for me at the end of this road, and this fills me with a selfish sort of dread, the same sort of selfishness which has brought me to this point.

Wipe the slate clean.

Erase me.

I am nothing.

I am no one.

Out of the corner of my eye, I see her again. She won't quit. She follows me wherever I go, pointing with her deformed fingers, all pale and grotesque. Her flesh, so white and pale, has rotted, hanging from her body like loose clothing, and her mouth hangs open as she continues to point.

Those eyes.

Those blood red eyes.

They follow me wherever I go. They see through me.

What is the point of this life? If God doesn't exist, if there is no heaven or hell, then our lives are simply an insignificant series of events which culminate in... in what? Lord knows I don't believe in any higher power, so what am I to make of this existence which I seem so inconveniently caught up in?

And all these thoughts swirl in my head like water funneling down a drain, all twisted and chaotic, as I contemplate what is worse; living a lie, or dying alone?

Monday

"Markus!"

My beloved wife, Tracy, is hollering at me from her tiny home office located in what used to be a closet beneath our staircase. Her voice reminds me of a rake being scraped over a chalkboard.

I stuff another bite of eggs into my gaping mouth and respond with a groan. The morning sun flitters through the window above the sink, landing upon our kitchen table in tiny pencils. The snow had finally melted away, giving birth to that early spring illusion of warm weather just around the corner. I watch the flecks of sunlight dance upon my generically tiled kitchen floor, and I feel nothing.

"It's Doctor Von Haymen on the phone. He'd like to speak with you!"

I shift in my chair, the worn-down bottoms scraping against the ceramic floor. Cringing at the sound, I crack my back with a grunt. We were long overdue for some new chairs. We needed a new laundry machine as well, probably could use a new fridge on top of that, and certainly the roof needed some work...

Of course, we were long overdue for a lot of things, including sexual intercourse (and it doesn't help matters that my wife is seven months pregnant).

"Tell him I can't come to the phone," I call back to Trace, whom is undoubtedly working on her latest novel, her belly swelling over the waistband of her stretch-pants in a grotesque orb. "Tell him I'm sick,"

"If you're sick, then Doctor Von Haymen is exactly the person you should be talking to!"

4

"Tell him I'm destitute, that we've got no money."

"Healthcare is free in Canada, Markus. You know this."

"Is it?"

I saw Doctor Von Haymen a month ago, and when he mentioned a slight abscess on my testicle, well, let's just say I have no inclination to go back anytime soon to find out just exactly what's going on down there, because the minute I find out I have cancer, I am quite convinced that I will die almost instantly.

What I don't know can't kill me.

Flawed logic, I know, but hey, whatever works, right?

In the meantime, I can busy myself with the banalities of my predictable and hopelessly stagnant middle-aged life by refusing to admit that I have a drinking problem and pretending to still be in love with my wife.

Tracy sighs and I listen to her tell Doctor Von Haymen that I will call him back. It's 9:30am on a Monday and I simply do not have the patience or state of mind to even bother doing my dishes after breakfast, let alone deal with an abscess on my testicle.

I still have half an hour before I need to head into the office, so I proceed to the living room and collapse on our black leather couch, turning on the television and settling on CBC for a morning update. It's a fairly standard modern day set-up, hardwood floors and a dining room off to the side. We knocked down the wall separating the kitchen from the living room about a decade ago (a project which has lived on within my line of credit). I can hear Trace typing away on her computer, and each strike of the key is like a stake being stabbed through my eye. For some reason, I found her writing irritable beyond belief. Well, it wasn't entirely a mystery. I found her writing irritable because she was lousy at it. I felt embarrassed for her, but more so, for myself.

I stare back at the television where an overweight American politician is blabbering on about making the country great again. Those poor fuckers. What did the Romans say when their empire was crumbling? Somehow, I have a feeling it was quite similar to what this windbag is spewing. I guess that's what happens when your population has been systematically addicted to reality television and takes medical advice from TV doctors who advocate on behalf of miracle beans and magical sprouts.

At least it made for good entertainment.

In all honesty, I figured it was probably a good thing. Might as well get World War III over with. See where we stand after that (thinking about the impending destruction of humanity helps me deal with the thought of my impending bankruptcy). Looking around the living room, my gut hanging over my waistline like a deflated balloon (like all men, I am ceaseless and unabashed hypocrite), my green walls and hardwood floors (which are riddled with scratches from my dog's claws), it makes me wonder where the past twenty years have gone, and for a fleeting moment, I realize that if a bomb were to drop on this house and destroy every goddamn thing I owned, I don't think it would really bother me. In fact, it would be exhilarating. Freedom. Release. Let the bastards come!

I live in a rather large house in Orleans (not to brag), about twenty kilometres outside of the downtown core of Ottawa. I have venetian blinds on the windows, leather furniture and a 50' flat-screen up on the wall. There is a giant dark walnut dining table in our dining room that in all honesty is probably too big for the space we allocated for it, but whatever. Tracy has a large cabinet against the wall beside the giant walnut table, filled with fine china that we received on our wedding day; dishes that sit there never to be used, the light coating of dust symbolic of what has become of our marriage, and I am forced daily to fight off the temptation of taking a baseball bat and smashing every god-forsaken dish in that goddamn cabinet.

All the bedrooms are upstairs, and in the basement, we have our laundry room and another, smaller living room (which I use as my own personal whack-off dungeon).

I drive a four-door sedan and my wife used to drive a Rav4. We had to sell the Rav last year to help cover the cost of Tommy's tuition. We still haven't told him, partly because we don't want to make him feel guilty, but mostly because we are embarrassed for ourselves.

My closet is full of designer pants and dress shirts with too many buttons. I get them from a local tailor who I always make sure to tip $50 because it makes me feel superior and in-charge (even though I really can't afford to be tipping my tailor, let alone purchasing shirts that cost $250). In my profession, appearances are everything. Besides, the cloth is straight from Italy!

We have a Golden Retriever named Maximus who pisses himself whenever a guest comes over to the house, which is fine with me because we have hardwood floors and I make Tracey or Thomas attend to the daily piss puddles that appear in our front hallway. I refuse to clean the piss puddles because I never wanted a goddamn dog in the first place, and I certainly never wanted to name it Maximus. He is currently positioned beside me on the couch, and upon looking down, I am delighted to find a fresh coating of dog hair upon my freshly dry-cleaned dress-pants.

Trace moves past me and into the kitchen, heading towards the fridge, sighing loudly so that there's no way I can miss it. God, I loved it when she did that. It always quickened my resolve to continue doing whatever it was that was making her sigh audibly in that perfectly passive aggressive way that only a woman can master. I watch her move into the kitchen and turn my attention back to the television.

My wife has managed to stay in relatively good shape and is by all accounts still an attractive woman. I mean, yea there's some extra padding on her ass, but at least it didn't sag like a couple pieces of stale ham. You know, there's nothing worse than a middle-aged woman in a pair of Spanx, their ass all squished in looking like a lumpy sweater. Nope, Trace still had shape to her ass, which made it much easier to achieve erection on the odd occasion when we partook in marital relations.

People say she looks like Meryl Streep, and that may be true, but now-a-days all I see is a giant black blob with a fleck of red in it.

She has sandy blond hair, long legs, decent tits, and she only lets me inside her once a month. The sex is mediocre at best. She wasn't always a dead fish, but after twenty years of marriage, I guess the salmon gets tired of swimming up creek, if you know what I mean (and no, she doesn't give blowjobs anymore).

She is also fucking pregnant again, and I'm still having trouble figuring out just how in the hell that happened. I mean, for Chrissakes I can hardly make it up the stairs to our bedroom, and yet somehow my sperm managed to penetrate her ovaries. Like Thomas, this pregnancy was not planned nor expected. Why is it that life always chooses your most vulnerable moments to throw you a curveball? I mean, ten years ago this would have been fine. We could have handled it ten years ago, before the crash of 2008, back when people still had faith in the housing market. But no, of course not, the storks elected to wait for me to be at my lowest point financially since just after university to bestow another giftwrapped blessing upon my humble household. Fucking storks.

Just think about what another child is going to do to her...

Her breasts are already sagging from the boy, and I can't imagine what her nipples are going to look like after this next little bastard gets his teeth latched on. She used to have quite nice breasts, to be honest, but life is a goddamn train wreck – especially for women. (I assume the baby will be a boy because I cannot fathom the idea of raising a little girl).

On top of all that, I am a hypochondriac and I'm convinced that I've contracted anal warts from my mistress (who is also married and whose husband is our local Member of Parliament and probably has anal warts as well). If it's not anal warts, then I probably have bowel cancer, or prostate cancer, or any other type of cancer that you can think of – somehow, I'm sure that I have it all (although I am far too scared to actually go to the doctor and find out for sure).

So now maybe you can understand why I simply cannot stomach the thought of speaking with Doctor Von Haymen.

Goddamn it feels great to be forty!

Well, forty-six if I'm being honest; a forty-six-year-old Real Estate Agent with a baby on the way whose ambitions died along with the Y2K scare (sorry to all you millennials who have absolutely no clue what the fuck Y2K is).

It doesn't help matters that my pregnant wife is no longer working, leaving me the soul financial provider for the family, which is rather hilarious in a sick and twisted sort of way, considering I am just about the worst financial planner in the history of numbers. I have two Visas, both of which are maxed out, a line of credit that I dip into on a far-too-frequent basis, a mortgage that still has ten fucking years left on it, a son who is currently attending Queen's University in Kingston (on my fucking dime), and a rather prominent drinking problem that I have yet to address. So, yeah; retirement is nowhere in sight.

Trace used to be a teacher. She used to have passion and ambition and all that other shit. We were bringing in over three hundred thousand annually with our combined salaries back then, if only we had managed to save any of it. Tracy had to take a leave of absence from teaching because of all the panic attacks she was having. And no, she did not work long enough to earn that sweet, sweet teacher's pension that everyone asks about. I almost felt sympathy for her, but my resentment towards my own life is so palpable that it is sadly impossible for me to feel any sort of empathy towards her.

She spends most of her time now trying to write romance novels (and it pains me to tell her that her writing is lousy and clichéd). I will come home from work and she will ambush me with pages from her latest novel (she has about four now, all of which end with the woman protagonist leaving her husband for her true love). Then she will sit down across from me at the kitchen table and stare straight into my tethered soul while I read her worn out prose.

She has also recently discovered Facebook, which is a downright torture upon me. Her friend Natalie, who was always so concerned about staying relevant, had turned her onto it a few weeks ago, and she'd been pretty much addicted to the Book ever since.

It was a dangerous thing, giving something like Facebook to my wife, a forty-five-year-old pregnant woman with no job and a social life that was pretty much non-existent. She now had a nasty habit of compulsively comparing her life to the pictures of her

9

friends on Facebook (all thirty-three of them, the poor woman). She had yet to fully grasp the fact that 99% of what people put on the internet is complete and utter bullshit. It was a strange phenomenon really, watching her try to navigate this new digital world.

It defied logic, in a lot of ways. I mean Photoshop has been around for decades now, and yet my wife still wants to look like the women in magazines, or in Youtube commercials, even though she knows they're not really women. Not real women, anyways.

But, hey – what do I know? I'm just another overweight middle-aged white man, after all.

The spoiled gender and race combined.

Public Enemy Number Fucking One.

Because, who do you blame for the famine in Africa? The white man. What about slavery in America? Right again. Persecution of Muslims? Oh, you better fucking believe that's me. And don't even get me started on whose responsible for the objectification and subjugation of women...

The Western Caucasian Man, the greatest monster in human history.

"Markus, don't you have to get going?"

"Yes, yes," I say.

I kiss Trace on the cheek on my way past and make for the front voyeur, slipping on my leather shoes from Harry Rosen, and I am swiftly out the door, the stale taste of my wife's sweat dancing upon my leather tongue. I stroll on out to our mailbox perched at the edge of our lawn by the street. My neighbor, who has lived beside me for ten years, waves at me as he enters his own car. I wave back and try to remember his name. Steve... no, Brian? Whatever.

I flip the little red flag on the mailbox down and pull the latch open. A bundle of envelopes comes spilling out onto the street, and stooping down I scoop up the various overdue bills that have accumulated on this lovely Monday morning. Let's see; mortgage payment, two months past due. Visa card, three months past due. There's a letter from a collections agency that is no doubt asking for payment on my life insurance policy. I'm sure those bastards will continue to send me overdue bills even after I'm dead. Dear Mr. Stanfield, in light of your recent death, we find it imperative that you contact us and arrange payment for your overdue account...

It wouldn't surprise me.

I have a sneaking suspicion that the entire institution of marriage is merely an elaborate ploy designed to drain any semblance of individuality and enjoyment from my bones. To cajole me. To twist and shake and bend me until I finally snap. Spend. Debt. Repeat. Sex. Marriage. Wedding. Debt. Mortgage. Car. Sex. Kids. University. Debt. Debt. Debt. DEBT!

Anyone see a pattern developing here?

I pop open the trunk of my four-door sedan and deposit the bundle of envelopes under the spare tire, along with the rest of them. They were starting to pile up now, and it might be necessary to have a little backyard bonfire in the coming weeks.

My name is Markus Stanfield, I'm forty-six years old and my life is a sick joke.

My nineteen-year-old son, Thomas, who is studying English Literature (despite my machinations and overhanded warnings), is coming home for Easter this weekend and I can't begin to tell you how uncomfortable and anxious I am awaiting his inevitable arrival. We don't really see things the same way. Never have. I can remember long meals of unsolicited silence, staring at each other's plates rather than making any real human connection. God forbid we looked into each other's eyes. Kids these days were more comfortable staring at their cell phone screens anyways.

I used to try to find common interests with Thomas, but gave up a few years ago when I realized that we legitimately have nothing in common, and overall our experiences together have been forced and mundane. He has never liked the music that I've showed him over the years, and I certainly can't stand the shit he listens to.

I made Thomas sign up for hockey when he was ten, and it took me a considerable amount of effort to pry him away from his goddamn Xbox, or computer, or fridge (anywhere in the house for that matter), whenever he had a practice or a game. Was it always like this? At least when I was growing up we played board games, or card games, you at least needed to be with other people. Nowadays it seems like everything can be done alone, and I don't think my son gives a shit about whether he is with anyone else or not. I used to hate being alone – I still do, which is ironic in a sick sort of way because I also can't stand spending any extended amount of time at home with my family.

Anyways, the whole hockey experiment lasted a total of two years before Thomas broke down and Trace forced me to allow him to quit. And he's been sitting on his computer ever since.

I do not understand my son.

He was never scared of thunder storms or getting cancer. He's always been more scared of getting bombed. He has a Threat Monitor App on his cell phone which notifies him of any change to his imminent safety through a colour coded system that doesn't really make sense to me (isn't orange more threatening than yellow?), and he used to come running into the kitchen sometimes, waving his phone in the air and screaming, 'We just got upgraded to Status Red!'

He used to get scared whenever an airplane or helicopter would fly overhead (and this happened quite frequently, being that we live in Ottawa). Up until he was twelve or thirteen years old. He would wrench his neck back all wide-eyed and frantic, staring up into the sky as if it were about to fall.

"What's happening?"

"It's just a plane."

"What if it's Al-Qaeda?"

"It's not Al-Qaeda."

"How do you know? What if it's the Russians, or the Chinese?"

"Well, then I suppose we are in big trouble."

And he would look up at me with wide eyes and a trembling lip, and I can't help but admit that it breaks me up to see his lip tremble, not solely because I feel the need to protect him, but because I was ashamed of that goddamned lip – the trembling lip that I created.

"It's not the Russians, and it's not the Chinese. Jesus, what are they teaching you in school?"

"Do you know that the United States owes China trillions of dollars? Our Western economies are on the verge of collapsing..."

"Trust me son, we are a long way from that – and the U.S. may owe China a lot of money, but they also have a lot of guns and naval ships and fighter jets. Besides, you shouldn't worry about that stuff, because if anything actually does happen, it will happen so fast that all of us will be obliterated before we even know what the hell is going on, so just relax."

And as the boy got older, the further away we became. He questioned things, which I guess made me proud in a certain way, but also annoyed and infuriated me, because he was just like every other kid from the warless generation; full of liberal ideologies that lacked the harsh filter of reality. By the time he was sixteen, he was a full on truther...

"We can't win a war on terror," he would tell me over dinner.

"Of course we can't," I would retort.

"Well, then why are we in a war if we can't win?"

"Because son, they don't want to win. They don't ever want it to end, you see?"

"But that doesn't make any sense!"

"Oh sure it does, boy. Think about it. You just don't understand freedom yet. And by freedom, I mean capitalism."

"Dad, why can't you take anything seriously?"

"I am being serious!"

But by the way he would shake his head and look down at his plate, I could always tell that he didn't believe me. He had given up on me, discarded me for the bitter old pessimistic man that I was (shit, I guess I can't really blame him on that one).

Tracy used to insist that I attempt to bond with Thomas, that I start initiating more mutual activities for us to participate in together.

"But Tracy, he doesn't want to go anywhere with me."

"Yes, he does," she would insist. "Thomas, don't you want to go with your father?"

13

And Thomas would look from me to his mother, back and forth, trying to gauge which one of us was more emotionally distraught over his pending answer, and of course, my wife almost always win this battle.

"Yeah, I want to be with you dad."

"Okay then, let's go golfing."

"I don't feel like golfing."

"Well what about tennis? We could go play tennis."

"My elbow hurts after..."

"That's called tennis elbow son, and it's something that fat old men are supposed to be struggling with, not sixteen-year-old boys."

"Markus! Don't talk to him like that."

"Okay, okay, what would you like to do then?"

"I dunno," he would shrug, "there's nothing to do, I guess."

"Nonsense," Trace would pipe in, "there's plenty to do. Why don't you guys go down by the canal and watch the boats coming through? Or you could take one of those boat cruises out onto the Ottawa River and learn a thing or two, maybe stop by the Parliament Buildings? I mean, we live in this beautiful city full of so much history, and I don't think you boys ever get to experience any of it! You could take him to the Museum of Civilization, or maybe the Art Gallery, I hear there is an absolutely breathtaking exhibit on Van Gogh!"

"I'm trying to bond with the boy, not turn him gay."

"Markus!"

"I know, I know, I'm sorry."

I used to worry that my son was going to be gay. It was something that filled me with a shameful sort of dread, because it's not supposed to matter, but it does (and anyone who tells you different either has a gay child, or doesn't have children to begin with). It matters. I used to think I would be ashamed of my gay son, like I am ashamed of his trembling lip, but now I'm not so sure. Now I think I would prefer it if he were gay. At least then he wouldn't have to put up with the constant badgering and unanswerable questions that come along with women. The irritations of being with someone who always assumes the worst of you, is never upfront about how they feel, and can somehow always tell when you are lying. My wife has a sixth sense when it comes to picking up on my dishonesty, she does it with such ease that I hardly even bother lying to her anymore.

"Where have you been all night?" she will ask.

"I was out drinking with Richard. We stopped at the strip club after work and drank shots of whiskey until I finally decided to call up my mistress and meet her at the Minto Suites..."

"Oh Markus, you're such a tease – let's take that sassy attitude upstairs."

And yet again my attempts to destroy her end in vain, and I am forced to begrudgingly climb the stairs behind her, taking all my strength and focus to lift one foot in front of the other, clutching the railing with white knuckles and grinding my teeth because as I follow her up the stairs I hear the faint sound of air being pushed out towards me, and I hear her laugh and say 'oops, a little tootsie,' which makes me nearly jump headfirst back down the stairs, ready to accept any sort of oblivion or sanctuary there is to offer. Oblivion or sanctuary, I couldn't care less, as long as it isn't this place.

Our nine-year-old dog (that's sixty-three in dog years) is going blind and also pees on the floor whenever a guest comes over to the house. His name is Maximus because Tracy has an unhealthy infatuation with Russell Crowe, which is fine with me since I happen to have an unhealthy infatuation with any female other than my wife. Sometimes I will come home from work, and upon opening the door I will hear a significant thud as I swing it inside the house, and Maximus will let out a weak yelping sound, bounding off down the hall, looking back at me with scornful eyes that say 'you used to love me'.

"Are we going to get a new puppy?" my son used to ask.

"We still have a dog now, in case you forgot."

"He doesn't do anything though, he just lies there all the time – and pisses himself."

"Sounds familiar, do you remember anything from when you were a baby?"

15

"That's not fair," he would say. "You can't blame me for pissing myself when I was a baby."

"Sure I can, just as much as you can blame the dog for pissing himself because he's old. It's a cycle son, you are born and you are completely and utterly dependent on your family, and when you get old and senile, guess what, you better hope you've got some family left! That's why your mother and I decided to have you – we wanted to make sure there was someone around who could change our diapers."

"That's fucking disgusting dad," he would say, grinning because he is smart enough to understand my sarcasm, although I'm sure he would rather not talk about such things. I enjoyed being a cynic around him – shit, I might as well be, the world was a cynical enough place to get used too – I am merely training him, molding him into a gladiator (yea, yea, I know – fucking Russell Crowe), who will take on the world with a head of steam, until his body grows old and his bladder is no longer able to control itself. What a sick, twisted cycle we live through – nature was always so blunt about reminding us too – the seasons, the clock, the orbit of the earth around the sun – everything is circular, and everything seems pointless to me.

My dog, who is named Maximus and pees himself whenever he gets excited, is also an alcoholic. He will roam about the house in search of open beers and mix drinks left unattended (which is usually pretty easy to find if I'm home) and he doesn't just take a couple sips either, no, the fucker will drink my entire drink, spilling it onto the floor and mopping up the sticky remains with his tongue. He will jump up onto my lap in a vain attempt to trick me, and while I gently pet behind his ears, he will lean down and steal my drink right out of my hand. Eventually he will become so inebriated that he starts to stumble, walking around with his head lolling from side to side, tripping over his own feet and drooling.

The poor pooch was on his last legs, that was a certainty.

"Dad! I think Maximus just fell down the stairs."

"Again?"

"He's not moving."

16

I turn from the TV and look over towards the landing where Maximus is all sprawled out on the hardwood floor, panting with his tongue lolling out from the side of his gaping mouth.

"He's fine," I say. "He's just resting."

"I think he's drunk," my son says.

I look down into my glass and see a good amount of dog hair swirling around within the dark brown liquid, and realizing that I am completely helpless to fight against any of these meddlesome frustrations, I shrug and slug back the rest of my drink, cringing and coughing.

That night, after Tracy has fallen asleep, and I, unable to sleep because of my pregnant wife's constant flatulence (after twenty years of marriage there was very little shame left in either of us, the farts flew freely), her hips brushing up against me as she thrashes about, rolled from bed and shuffled downstairs to the living room, collapsing on the couch and flicking on the television. It's 3:22am and there isn't really anything worth watching except sports highlights. I make an executive decision to get up off the couch and pour myself a nice scotch.

I get back to the couch and collapse into the middle cushion. There is a dull throbbing pain behind my eyes and I rub at them until I see stars. The scotch helps. Maximus stirs from the front hallway. He notices me on the couch and instantly heads towards the stairs so that he can steal my place in bed beside Tracy. Typical.

My wife's new novel is sitting in a scattered pile on our coffee table, and I snatch up one of the pieces of paper and bring it in close to my face, the glow from the TV emitting barely enough light to read it:

Natasha watches the mailman approach through the front window, her senses keenly alert all of a sudden, and she touches her lips, brushing them softly with her fingertips. What if she invited him in, his broad shoulders, much broader than her husband's, his flat stomach and muscular arms, and he would know how to treat a lady, he would be generous and caring and gentle. There is a flutter inside her as she moves to get a view of the mailman inserting the envelopes into her slot...

Jesus.

A commercial flashes across the television screen showing young women with large breasts and small waists who probably don't fart and roll around like animals in their sleep (and even if they do, who gives a shit). A phone number is blinking at me from the bottom of the screen in big white numbers, and because the commercial is sort of making my dick hard right now, mixed with the fact that I can't sleep and my head is still throbbing, I decide to give them a call, even though I've never called a sex line before in my life.

I reach out for the cordless phone on the coffee table and dial the 1-800 number.

While I wait for somebody to answer I can feel my heart beating against my chest with every nerve-racking ring that goes unanswered. Did this make me a hopeless pervert? Was I some sort of deranged stalker type that was on the brink of going on a prostitute killing rampage... I guess it's hard to say.

"Hello?" a scandalously clad voice answers.

"Uh, hi, err, how are you?"

"I'm fine sweetie. Do you want to talk for a bit?"

"Okay," I say.

"Well, I'll need your credit card number, its $5.99 a minute, or ten minutes for $50," and it's amazing how quickly her demeanor has changed from horny to professional, sex to business. I guess there wasn't all that much of a difference between the two, when you got right down to it.

"Just give me the ten minutes."

I tell the girl my credit card number (with a gnawing anxiety in my gut telling me that my identity will surely be stolen, although in all honesty, I would feel bad for the poor sap who inherits my mountain of debt – it would undoubtedly ruin his life), and after the payment is all out of the way, the girl starts talking in that very low, sexy voice that she answered the phone with in the first place.

"So," she says, "what's your name, babe?"

"It's, huh, Roger."

"Well, hello there, Roger. Do you like wet pussy?"

18

"I don't hate it."

"Hmm, good – I want you to touch my wet pussy, I want you to bite my nipples..." and she is breathing heavier now, her raspy voice beginning to crack, and all I can picture is a four-hundred-pound woman with a pony tail crammed into an office chair eating a goddamn Snickers bar and drinking can after can of Diet Pepsi (why is it that the fat people are always the ones drinking Diet Pepsi?)

"Can I stop you there?" I interrupt.

"What's the matter, babe?"

"It's just – did you know that our economy lost 45,000 jobs last month?"

"Um, no sweetie, I didn't know that."

"Well it's true, and it's not good – because we just finished handing out stimulus a couple years ago, and if the surge we pushed through our economy is already over, well, then we're in big trouble. And that really doesn't bode well for my business, considering the housing market will likely collapse along with the economy. Not to mention the fact that interest rates are undoubtedly going up in the next quarter, which will put significant stress on an already overburdened housing market. People can't be buying houses when they can't afford dinner, you see? Meanwhile, the States just elected a bumbling fool in a hair piece as their fucking president, and the European Union is on the verge of separating, which will open the door for Russia or China, or both. I mean, what are these politicians thinking? Sometimes, I think all of them are disconnected with reality – completely brainwashed by the system, and it's not their fault – I mean, the system is key – we need the system. Without the system, we'd all be hacking into each other's skulls, we'd be animals – you see the thing is; I can't stand it when I watch people blindly swallow the mandates and bits of half-information that is fed to them from above. I mean, think for your selves' goddamnit, you know? Sometimes I just feel like those calling the shots have no idea what it's like to be the average person, to be a normal guy or girl. Everything is slipping, we're beginning to digress, just like in the U.S. – our political system is changing. There are the haves and the have-nots. The Prime Minister was never supposed to have as much influence and power over caucus as he does now – just as the President of the United States wasn't supposed to be polarized. I guess we just like making celebrities out of ourselves... when it all comes down to it, everyone wants power, and in our superficial society, we've all become narcissists. A bunch of self-perpetuating Napolenes running around on our horses made of debt. Oh, and did I mention that I think my son might be gay?"

I wait for her to respond, for the sound of her heavy breathing, anything – but the line is dead, that soft nothingness filling up my skull until another faceless and robotic voice tells me to hang up and try again.

The next morning I awake on the couch all sprawled out with my legs hanging off the opposite end. Maximus is sitting directly beside me and has been lapping at my face for lord knows how long. I can feel his drool all wet and sticky on my cheeks, and as I push the dog away from me, I notice that my once half-full scotch glass is now empty, and there is a good amount of dog hair stuck at the bottom of the cup.

You were licking my pours clean, you goddamn alcoholic.

My back feels like a pretzel as I pull myself up into a sitting position. I look over at Maximus whose mouth is twisted back in a taunting grin, sitting there panting and looking quite pleased with himself.

"You little bastard," I say.

My wife complains to me about her feminine itching. And it's beyond me why she feels the need to tell me about it, but regardless, I have to sit there and rub her feet because the pregnancy causes them to become all swollen and sore, and she will insist that we watch some sort of mindless reality show on TV, and pretty much all of them seem the same to me – a bunch of hopeless fucks attempting to get famous – and my wife will say things like 'can you believe that woman?' and I will say, 'no, it's unbelievable,' but really I'm just thinking about how soon she will develop Type

II Diabetes so that her eye sight will fail completely and I am no longer subjected to such torment.

"I think I have bowel cancer," I will say.

"Well, why don't you go to the doctor?"

"Not a chance – there's no way. What I don't know can't kill me."

"When's the last time you had a colostomy?"

"I don't know... when I was thirty-five, I guess."

"Even if you do have cancer, the only way to beat it is by early detection. Haven't you seen those commercials? They can treat a lot of it now. Medicine has come a long way. You take some treatments, some chemotherapy and you'll be fine."

"I'd rather die."

And then she will get upset, wrenching her swollen feet from my grip and storming upstairs to our bedroom, and I will sit there feeling miserable and guilty for causing her such grief, so much so that I end up pouring a couple glasses of red wine and cutting up some cheese to bring up to the bedroom, and she will be lying there on our bed watching the same reality show that was on downstairs in the living room, and when she sees me standing in the doorway with the wine and cheese she will smile and gesture for me to come to her.

"You're so sweet," she will say to me, stuffing her mouth full of cheese and wine, and watching her chew, that incessant mushing sound, the way the cheese sits all yellow and curdled on her tongue, it makes me sick so that I end up guzzling the wine down until I am drunk, which hardly offers any sort of relief because she gets mad at me for drinking (especially now that she is pregnant and cannot also get drunk). She never used to get mad at me for being drunk, not until she got pregnant that first time. As soon as that first child comes along, it's like a switch gets flicked on inside the head of a woman, and suddenly, any sort of fun that I want to have is an affront to her because she cannot partake. Women develop a certain sort of self-entitled bitterness after having a child, so I've noticed. It's a slippery slope, and even after the baby pops out, that jealousy remains within her bones as she continues her crusade to prevent me from having any semblance of a happy and free life.

21

This new pregnancy is torture on me.

She doesn't want me to be able to drink because she is not able to drink. It's been six months since she's had a drink and as the days slip by it infuriates her all the more watching me drink. She aims to suck any remaining youth from my bones, and I have a sneaking suspicion that she got pregnant again on purpose, to finally ruin me and dash any hopes of escape that I may have had.

"This pregnancy was a blessing in disguise," she will say, "it's going to bring us so much closer." And by the way she sits there across the table from me with her chin in her hand, smiling that naïve smile and batting her eyelashes, it drives me almost to the point of insanity, because I can see that she actually believes it. Does she not know the stats for having children after forty? The odds of having a mentally defected child go from 1 in 1500 in your twenties to something like 1 in 60 in your forties. It pains me because she still loves me very much and somehow, she remains completely oblivious to my emotional detachment. We were never planning on having another child, I didn't think it was even possible to be honest; otherwise I would have been double-wrapping my cock whenever we were in the same room together. But no, you had to be a bone head, diving in head first with no form of contraception at all (which is also a habit I have with my mistress). My worst nightmare is that the baby will come out a girl. Having a son was hard enough, but at least I can be crass with him, at least I don't have to worry about him getting pregnant or being fucked around all the time by horny little bastards, or naked pictures of him being posted across the internet. There was something daunting and terrifying about having a girl. For some reason I just don't think I could handle it, because if there was one plain and simple truth to my existence it was this; I don't understand women.

Tuesday

Like so many before me, after my aspirations, ideologies and whimsical positivity had been extinguished by the onslaught of student debt, an overly saturated job market, and rising inflation, I became a Real Estate Agent... because I wanted money, and I didn't want to go back to school to get it.

Real Estate in Ottawa is solid thanks to all the full pocketed politicians and bureaucrats who roam the streets, all dressed up in their firmly pressed button-down shirts, slowly suffocating themselves to death with neckties. When the housing bubble finally pops, and it's going to be one giant fucking pop, especially in places like Toronto and Vancouver, Ottawa's Real Estate market will still be standing tall, because even during recessions, there is always still one entity that has an abundance of money: the government.

I started my Realtor career working with Royal Lepage. I stuck it out with them for ten solid years, building my client list and learning the does and don'ts of the profession. It's not small, it's cozy, or, this is an up and coming neighborhood (which of course is code for you are about to move into the fucking ghetto). And of course, I learned the importance of having a reliable and morally flexible mortgage broker. I got my Real Estate License when I was twenty-nine, and every year since then seems to have moved faster than the last. I sold my first house when I was thirty and spent my entire commission on cigars, booze, expensive dinners at fancy restaurants, and one new suit.

I hated working at Royal Lepage. There was always some keener wanting to waste my time with some sort of PowerPoint presentation. I can always tell how much I will hate a person by how enthusiastic they are about PowerPoint presentations. Everyone is always trying to prove their worth in today's overly saturated workforce. It's pathetic. I'm not sure who I hate more; the baby-boomers who should have long since retired, but thanks to the past few decades of reckless spending and pension cash outs, cannot; or the millennial douchebags fresh from university who like to stress the importance of social media and say words like environmental sustainability far too much.

After ten years of working with Royal Lepage, and dealing with thousands of stubborn, pigheaded, overly opinionated clients who always assumed they knew better than their Real Estate Agent, I started my own company and haven't had to deal with PowerPoint presentations or water cooler small talk since then, thank the fucking lord Jesus.

I usually get into the office at around 9:15am. It's located downtown just off the 417 in a strip mall on the corner of Metcalfe and Gladstone. The walls are beige and the carpet is green. It has the stale look and smell of pretty much every goddamn strip-mall office in the world. There's a receptionist area tucked into the back corner of the first room, where an empty desk greets my clients.

The subtle hum of the computer haunts me.

I hang my jacket up on the rack at the front and make my way past the empty reception desk which has yet to be graced with a receptionist since I began leasing the two-room office the better half of a decade ago.

Moving into the back room where my actual office is set-up, I sit down in my stained rotating computer chair behind my burgundy oak-wood desk. My wrists crack as I jam my password into the keyboard and pull up my Inbox.

At this point, it's time for my coffee.

I go over to the Tassimo machine I keep on top of the filing cabinet and pop the lid, placing one of the pucks of coffee into the opening. As it brews I check the scores from last night's hockey games, and see that the Leafs lost, again, and so I'm out fifty bucks on a bet I made online.

Fuck.

The finished coffee fills my nostrils and I snag the cup out from the machine and return to my computer. For the next twenty minutes I cruise the internet: video of gorilla attacking family at the zoo on Youtube (fully watched); article on the war in the Middle East highlighting the costs and casualties thus far (half-read); article on murdered pornstar who was found dead in her home last night (fully read); sports article on the Leafs and how this year's season was yet another disappointment (three quarters read); another Youtube video (half-watched); article on how to cook bacon-wrapped steaks on the barbeque (fully read).

I sigh and push myself back from the keyboard, reaching for my notebook which has the names and numbers of potential clients I have told myself I would cold-call for the past month and a half, but have yet to dial a single digit.

Business has been, for lack of a better word - nonexistent - as of late. The goddamn newspapers keep prattling on about a housing bubble, and the feds have made it clear that interest rates will be remaining at the very same miniscule level of 2.5% for the next foreseeable future, which has removed all urgency from homebuyers. I haven't closed a deal in over four months, not for a lack of trying. It was typical though, considering we were two and a half years into a new government, all of the new political androids who came pouring into the city two years ago are all well and settled. Ottawa was a funny city that way. Everything moved in cycles predicated on the government. In another year or so things would pick up, but no politician or staffer in their right mind would ever purchase a home with an election looming just over a year away. It's just not sound economic policy, you see?

And what do they call betting money on sporting events?

Shut-up.

And you bet on the Leafs? You might be economically autistic.

There's nothing worse than a sarcastic subconscious.

I have a grand total of one client at the moment. A single goddamn client.

And they were an incorrigible pain in my ass. But being that it was late Spring, coupled with the fact that the financial forecast for the coming year had most people petrified to buy houses, the Scholaces were my only clients.

The phone starts ringing and I glare at it as if the faceless-black phone is a stranger who has just walked in on me taking a shit. How dare you?

"Office of Markus Stanfield, how may I help you?"

The thought of hiring a secretary had crossed my mind, and even if it would make my life a whole helluva lot easier around here, I doubt I would able to help myself from dipping the company pen into her soft wet ink (obviously, I would hire a young woman for the job, I mean, I'm not an idiot).

"Marky boy!" a familiar voice rings in my ear. "Lunch beers?"

I sigh audibly and look up at the clock. 11:15. Close enough.

"Lion's Cock in twenty," he says, and hangs up.

I get to the Cock and Lion on Sparks Street (or Lion's Cock as we have so eloquently dubbed it), entering through the old wooden door and descending the steel steps caked with dirt, blood, puke, and what I can only assume is human shit. I see Dick sitting at the far end of the stale bar as I come bounding in through the red door at the bottom of the stairs. The lighting is dim and the seat cushions have that faded colour to them like a rotten lime.

It truly was the perfect bar for early afternoon drinking.

Dick's hair is greying, some of it is already white near the top of his head, and his goatee is also a greyish-white. Why any middle-aged man would choose to have a goatee is still beyond me, but hey, whatever you've got to do to convince yourself that you're still young, right? Dick had the average dad-body that the kids seemed so hot on these days. Broad shoulders, gut poking out the front of his buttoned shirt, flat ass and skinny legs. He also wore thick framed glasses because Dick has two cataracts and cannot see worth shit. All in all, he was utterly and unremarkably average. He basically looked like Hank Hill.

Which is probably what made him such a Dick.

"Mark!" he hollers over at me, waving his arm in the air. "Barkeep, please retrieve a cold pint for my friend here."

Dick is divorced (naturally). His ex-wife works in the Prime Minister's Office, which is pretty typical of most relationships on the Hill (politics is an incestuous business).

The youngish bartender with pink hair and piercings smiles with some effort and turns her back to retrieve a glass, and when I hear one of the hipster university students say, well it's just so like, draconian, you know?, I ponder the idea of dashing back up the stairs and out the door. Too late now.

Dick works for the Minister of Natural Resources, and he's worked in politics for over two decades now, which is a lot of time to spend eating shit. He's got his suit jacket hung over the back of his chair and I can see giant wet spots under his armpits seeping through the thin fabric of his dress shirt. God, being a middle-aged man was such a fucking train wreck.

I met Dick back when I worked on the Hill, when we were both kids in short pants carrying our boss's briefcases around and pretending to be important. He was my last remaining connection to the political world in Ottawa, and sadly, probably one of my only friends. It's a travesty that I mostly hated him.

"Dick, tell me something," I say, pulling up a stool beside him.

"Anything you ask, good-sir."

"If you were Prime Minister, would you name your cock the Right Honourable Member, or the Executive Branch?"

"Hmmm," he ponders, fingering the rim of his pint glass in earnest reflection. "I think I'd have to go with the Minister of Internal Affairs..."

"And you would sit on the Committee of the Whole, no doubt."

"Indeed," he says, raising his glass and downing a considerable amount of beer in one giant gulp.

"So, Markus," he says, wiping his lips and chin with the back of his hand. "What's up today? Any pending sales to boast about?"

"You know how the market is right now," I sigh. "Not a goddamn sale in sight."

"Ah," he sighs, "Real estate will bounce back. It always does."

"Yeah, that's what they said in 2008."

"Any troubles on the home front?"

27

Dick had an annoying tendency to poke and prod at your personal life. Since he was a politician, he almost always had advice to give on any godforsaken topic that you may so unfortunately happen to bring up. He was always trying to give me advice on how to run my business, which of course is ludicrous considering he's a fucking politician and so therefore doesn't know a goddamn thing about what running an actual business is like.

"All things are A-Okay on the home front, Dick. Thanks for asking."

"How's your pregnant wife?"

"She's still pretty fucking pregnant."

Richard laughs and pats me on the shoulder, "You're in for one helluva ride now, Marky-boy."

I grimace and take another drink from my beer.

"Do you know the stats on women giving birth after forty?"

"Of course I know the fucking stats," I say. "What? You think I haven't been checking the stats, do you think I haven't been dreading the idea of having a mongoloid child?"

"Okay, okay, easy does it big fella."

"It's either going to be a retard, or a girl, I just know it."

"Hey, that's not so bad," Dick says. "At least if your kid is mentally challenged, you'll never be the dumbest one in the room."

"Classy."

"Cheers," he says, nodding and slugging back the rest of his pint. He promptly orders another from the surly young bartender. She looked like the sort of young girl who had experienced one too many prick boyfriends in her short life, and had thus given up on shaving her still supple vagina.

"God, work has been torture today," Dick laments, laying his head into one of his sweat drenched palms.

"What's got you down at the office today, Dick?" I ask.

"Well," he begins, sighing deeply into the bottom of his now empty pint glass. "She's been a rough one. We're trying to get funding approved for the goddamn pipeline, but the cocksuckers at Transnational Oil & Gas won't take the goddamn money!"

"What do you mean?"

"Well, we've offered them a pretty enticing package... but TOG is stonewalling us."

"Sorry, let me get this straight... the government is trying to give a company free money, and they're refusing to take it?"

"Exactly. They don't want to adhere to the stipulations we are placing on the funds. All we are asking is that they spend 10% of the allocated funds on environmental protection."

"Seems fair."

"Not to them."

"So, what are you going to do about it, Dick?"

"Well, we have to get that goddamn pipeline built. It was part of our mandate for Chrissakes! And TOG is the only company capable of putting together enough capital to complete the project in a timely fashion. And the funny thing is, they don't really need our money so... they can sit on their hands and wait until Congress gives them funding from down south, and you can bet your bottom dollar those Yankees won't put any goddamn environmental stipulations on their funding. They really have our balls in a vice, I tell yea. Our solution at this point is to change provisions in the funding which force TOG to spend at least 10% of the allocated funds on hiring Aboriginal workers. We were hoping the fact they are natives might balance out the whole environmental thing..."

"There yea go Dick, looks like you saved the day!"

"Not quite," he grimaces. "The Abos don't want the jobs."

"Pardon me?"

"That's right. Those goddamn lazy Indians don't want to work for some multinational tree-killing water-polluting corporation. Those stupid fucks. Can't they see the opportunity, can't they see the common sense to it all?"

"Actually Dick, very little of this seems to make any sense..."

"Exactly!" he exclaims, slamming his fist on the bar counter. "Jesus, why can't the government just build the damn pipeline? It would sure as hell save me a whole helluva lot of stress."

"Oh, be careful there, Dick. That sounds like your advocating for government interference in private business. I believe they call that Communism..."

"Oh, fuck off."

"And I thought you were a good ol' Conservative?"

"I am," he insists, "but only when I'm not being a Communist."

Sometimes I like to fantasize about faking my own death.

I've already got the whole thing planned.

One lazy afternoon, I casually mention to my wife that I have the sudden urge to go canoeing. It wouldn't be the most absurd thing I've ever suggested. Back in my twenties I used to go canoeing quite often, when I still had the semblance of ambition and drive and all that bullshit that comes with being a clueless youth. Knowing that my pregnant wife would have absolutely no interest in joining me for such an activity (she's also deathly afraid of water), I would be in the clear. Once I got out into the river, it would be as simple as tipping over the canoe and swimming over to one of the riverbanks, allowing my poor, empty canoe to go rushing into the dam situated at the mouth of the Ottawa River. There would be no questions; a tragic accident, a man dead, a grieving widow and a son without a father.

We'd all be better off.

I arrive in my driveway, pulling in sharply and bringing the car to an abrupt halt. With the failure of yet another Open House, in which a total of five people showed up (four of them were just there for the free cookies and coffee, and the only real potential buyer was only there to compare neighborhoods), I am another step closer to bankruptcy.

It's been three months since I've been able to pay our mortgage. The car needs new brakes, and probably a new goddamn transmission as well, and on top of all of that, Tommy's tuition for next semester will be due in a month or so...

Maybe Trace will get one of her novels published...

The thought actually makes me laugh out loud (LOL!).

Or maybe I'll have that massive stroke I've been building up towards for the past twenty years. Although, that wouldn't really work either since I'm behind on my life insurance payments. Fuckers.

My house sits before me like a rotted tooth. I can see the roof needs to be re-shingled, and the gutters are overflowing with leafs and sludge. I try to think about the last time I was up there to clean them, and I realize that Trace has been the one taking care of that meddlesome task for the past decade.

Even the goddamn windows look all dirty and smudged from where I'm sitting, and I'm quite confident they haven't seen the nozzle-end of a Windex bottle for some time.

Husband of the year? I am not.

I need a drink.

On my way inside I check the mailbox, completely expecting it to be jam packed with unpaid bill notices. I observe with an odd sort of misgiving that the mailbox is empty. Void. All those French bureaucrats at the CRA must be on vacation.

It's a warm night for spring as the sun sets over the horizon, leaving a reddish-orange glow in the sky that makes me think of... well, nothing. It's the fucking sky. There's clouds. Birds chirping in the wind and all that garbage. Who gives a fuck? I'm in debt!

Did I mention I need a drink?

I walk in the front door, kicking my shoes off so that they land haphazardly in front of the white closet where Trace has told me about a million times to put my shoes. I notice the various paint chips in the wall from where the door knob comes smashing into contact every goddamn time somebody swings it open, and my ambivalence towards the damage seems to me a symptom of my reckless disregard for my family.

That's when I notice the pile of torn open envelopes sitting on the floor in the middle of the hallway. Maximus comes waddling over and stands by the ripped-up shreds of paper, looking up at me with his tongue lolling out and his head tilted slightly to the side.

Then I hear the sobbing.

Jesus sweet Mary-fucking Christ.

I make my way to the living room and find Trace curled up in a ball on the floor, rocking back and forth against the edge of the couch, her head lightly tapping the armrest with every back sway. She's got one of the bills clasped against her chest, hugging it against her with both arms like a dying infant. She has yet to

31

notice me, and I hear a guttural moan escaping her throat as she takes a moment to pause the sobbing in order to draw breath.

Maximus comes lolling up beside me, and he catches my eye as I peer down at him, the whites of his eyes showing as he looks up at me as if to say; what's with the this one, huh?

Your guess is as good as mine, brother.

"Sweetie," I say, stooping down, "what's wrong?"

"Oh, like you don't know!" she cries. "Look at these bills. LOOK AT THEM!" and she's screaming now, the tears streaming down her cheeks, "We are destitute, completely broke! You've been hiding this from me, Markus. How could you let this happen?"

"One bill at a time."

"Oh, you think this is funny?"

"Come on, Trace. We've been in tough spots before, it always works out. I'll sell a house and boom, we are good to go. This is just a bit of a... hump."

"How did the open house go then, huh?" she asks in defiance, looking up at me with eyes that glisten.

"Really good," I lie. "A lot of interest."

She smiles then, wiping at her cheeks and beginning the long and difficult ascent to her feet (hormones can work to your advantage the odd time). I reach down and help my pregnant wife up from the floor. Her belly swells out towards me like a balloon that's being pumped full of air.

"And how about the clients... what are their names again?"

"The Scholaces."

"Right," my wife nods. "Do you think they are getting close?"

"Oh yeah, they are ready. Any day now we will be closing on something."

Another lie.

The fucking Scholaces.

They were both accountants. Forensic accountants, no less. Which of course made them just about impossible to deal with. Oh, and did I mention they're Jewish?

Trace heads into the kitchen and I am left standing with Maximus, who continues to look up at me with those bulbous eyes. He paws at my leg and I can tell he has to go out so I take him over to the back sliding door and open it for him. He goes trotting out into our fenced in back yard and starts roaming. The phone rings in the kitchen and I hear Trace answer it.

"Markus!" she calls from the kitchen. "It's Doctor Von Heyman, he wants to speak with you."

"Tell him..."

"No! You can tell him whatever you like on your own."

Reluctantly, I make my way into the kitchen and take the phone from Tracy, sighing audibly into the mic.

"Hey Doc."

"Markus, how are you?"

"Well Doc, considering it's only Tuesday, not great. I'd be feeling much better if it was Friday. Hey! Is that something you could prescribe? A week full of Fridays would really do me good."

"How is your testicle feeling?"

"What about it?"

"Is it still causing you pain?"

"I never..."

"Tracy told me."

Treasonous whore!

"Well, you know... it hasn't been that bad lately."

"Mark, as I've said before, the key is early detection. We can treat many forms of cancer now with a high chance of success, but only if we catch it early enough."

"I know Doc, truly I do... it's just, I don't really have time to be sick right now, you know?"

"Don't be ridiculous..."

"It's not ridiculous! You doctors always act like we're being the crazy ones, but how in the hell am I supposed to deal with everything in my god-forsaken life on top of being sick? Surely the stress of going through treatment alone would kill me. I simply don't have time. And no one's ever sold a goddamn house looking like a bald radioactive mannequin man, Doc, and I desperately need to sell a goddamn house right now..."

"Markus..."

33

"I'm sorry Doc, look, I'll give you a call once I've got all this figured out."

"Mark, please you're also..."

"Wife's calling Doc, gotta go!"

I hang up with a grin and turn around to find Trace frowning at me, her eyes watering again. I start to say something but she runs off upstairs before I can get a word out. Whatever.

Wednesday

I'm sitting in my office staring at the wall. I usually leave Wednesday pretty wide open, because... well, because I fucking feel like it. It's nice to have a lazy day in the middle of the week. Besides the two showings I had in the early afternoon, my schedule is essentially wide open. I start scrolling through the news looking for something to peek my interest; dead babies, helicopter crashes, maybe an abduction or, god-willing, a terrorist attack that has killed and maimed hundreds.

Hey, I know what you're thinking. But don't blame me. I am merely a product of the media which bombards me.

I get a text from my AA sponsor Jim that reads; hey my man, will you be in attendance tonight at the meeting?

I respond with a resounding; yes.

Jim is an army veteran who did two tours over in Afghanistan. He suffers from post-traumatic stress disorder and has the uncanny ability of being able to drink an entire bottle of vodka in the early part of an evening. He also has a penchant for cocaine and pain-killers, and yet somehow, I am a constant disappointment to him.

Okay, I have that money for you, he responds.

It's been almost a year since I got my D.U.I.

I didn't actually get charged with anything, and to be honest, it wasn't really my fault. The goddamn Ontario government changed the limit from .8 to .5, and I ended up blowing .6, which was just enough for them to haul my ass into the station and suspend my license for thirty days. They slapped me with a Dangerous Driving charge too, just for the hell of it (or maybe because I was doing eighty in a forty), but I took the bastards

35

to court on that one. The judge sentenced me to a year's worth of Alcoholics Anonymous and removed the suspension on my license after reviewing my squeaky clean record (oh if they only knew the things I've done!).

Naturally, Tracy blew her lid when I called her from the cop-shop, but since I didn't end up losing my license, coupled with the fact that she believed Alcoholics Anonymous would be good for me, her anger subsided rather passively. She still made sure to take the odd jab at me though, whenever she was on the losing end of an argument, or when I happened to show up at home a bit drunk after work. She was good at twisting that particular knife. Neither of us have ever told Thomas about it, and to best of my knowledge, he still has no idea that his father spent a night sitting on the cold cement bench in the drunk tank. He just thinks I attend AA to better myself (HA!)

My cell phone vibrates against my desk.

"Hello?"

"Lunch beers?" Dick's voice vibrating in my ear.

"Done, see you at the Cock."

The Lion's Cock is surprisingly busy on this late Wednesday afternoon, mostly bureaucrats sitting in their suits, spewing Franglish from their crooked mouths. I had a special sort of hatred for bureaucrats. They worked as little as me, but had never put in the time or effort to earn their laziness. Why should they do anything more than the bare minimum? Oh God Bless our self-entitled modern-day society.

I find Dick posted up at our usual spot; tucked in at the corner of the bar – out of sight and out of our mind.

"So, Dick, what's the status on the pipeline?" I ask, taking a long and satisfying slug from my freshly poured beer.

"Big developments," he says, clapping his hands together. "We've scrapped the offer to TOG, those greedy fuckers. They can wait around and see if that Democratic President sends them a single goddamn cent for a pipeline. In the meantime, we've offered the funding to another company."

"Oh yeah? Which company is that?"

"The China National Petroleum Corporation."

"Dick... are you fucking joking me?"

"Do I look like I'm joking?"

"Is that not the state-owned oil company... from China?"

"Give this man a medal!" Dick says, clapping me on the back like it's the funniest thing in the goddamn world.

"But... so, what? We're handing over Canadian work, Canadian jobs, Canadian money... to a state-owned Communist corporation?"

"Oh, they'll still hire Canadians, I think. At least some, anyways. That's not the issue though."

"What's the issue?"

"They want to renegotiate our Foreign Investment Promotion and Protection Agreement."

"Okay... what the hell does that mean?"

"Tariffs," he sighs. "They don't want to pay them."

"Well, naturally."

"But they want to keep their own tariffs on our exports..."

"Sounds like a pretty fair deal."

"You don't get it Markus. This pipeline is everything to our Party. We have to get this fucker built before the next election or we are toast!"

"But, won't people get mad about the whole, China gets to export for free but Canada still pays tariffs to China... thing?"

Dick laughs heartily, lifting his beer to his lips and chugging deeply. "Markus, you nitwit. Canadians don't understand tariffs. They don't have a fucking clue!"

And that right there is why I had to leave politics.

"Time for another?"

"Nope, I'm gonna be late for AA."

My AA meetings occur every Wednesday night at the Wilfred Laurier High School for Adults on Lyon Street. I had driven past the sign on their front lawn many times, the one that read: AA Meetings every Wednesday Night: Together we are Strong, and I used to laugh at the poor bastards, sitting in that brightly lit gymnasium together, pretending to believe in God and all that

37

other crap they purported would help to heel their members (from my experience, the only thing that can do that is Penicillin). I make a point of having at least two drinks before each meeting, sometimes right in the parking lot of the school. I will sit in my car with the windows up and slug back a couple beers, pretty much begging the cops to roll up again (although, the parking lot of an AA meeting has got to be the last place they would think to check – I mean, nobody could be that stupid, right?). The whole ordeal is tiresome (it used to be bothersome, but I've come to find great irony in the entire situation, because since I've started coming to AA meetings I seem to be drinking even more).

I pull into the lonely parking lot, speckled with battered sedans driven by mostly single white men, and park near the back away from the rest of the cars. I didn't bring any beer with me this week, but I managed to have a couple rye and cokes in my office before leaving work, and combined with the lunch beers I had with Dick, I have developed an adequate enough buzz to comfortably endure the next two hours.

The school is a hulking shadow as I approach the propped open doors of the gymnasium, the light from inside spilling out into the evening gloom like an unwelcomed stain.

Inside, the gymnasium is lit up and there are rows of chairs set facing the back wall, the mesh from the basketball net swaying aimlessly above the podium. It smells of aftershave and cologne. There is a fold out table with coffee and Timbits set-up against the far wall, and I make my way there in order to pour myself a black coffee. There are probably forty people in the gym and they all look lost. Some of them fain smiles and laugh loudly, while others hunch over when they walk and have deep wrinkles and shaky hands; they don't laugh loudly.

As I'm sitting down a muffled belch escapes my throat, the lingering taste of whiskey swimming upon my tongue. A man with a long beard turns around in his seat, shakes his head at me, and then returns his gaze to the front. Fuck you very much, bud.

The instructor, or whatever you want to call him, approaches the mic to begin the meeting. His name is Tony and he's been

38

sober for ten years (poor bastard). He always wears a checkered dress shirt tucked into jeans, and for some reason I can't help but categorize him as one giant phony.

"Hello everyone, glad to see you all here. I see we have a few new faces here tonight, so how about starting them off right? Jim, would you mind?"

Jim rises and approaches the microphone rousing an applause from our fellow addicts. He was definitely the prized pupil. Everyone seemed to love Jim, and after almost fifty weeks of this bullshit, I don't think he's skipped a chance to share once. There is an air of anxiety and tension pulsating throughout the room, materializing itself in the form of constant sighs and restless legs.

"Hello everyone," he says, "thank you for letting me be here," he pauses, taking a gulp. I see that he's freshly shaved, no longer sporting his beard, and while this may sound like a good thing, it is usually a sign that Jim has just recently come off a rather stupendous bender in which he feels the need to start over again. I know this because he told me.

"It's been three years since Geoff killed himself..." Jim bows his head and pauses for a moment. "We served overseas together, Geoff and I, and if you're a regular attendee to these meetings, you will recognize the name... I've talked about him plenty of times before..." he pauses again while others in the crowd make coughing noises and scratch their necks. "So, yea... today is the anniversary... I can still remember... walking into his apartment, still drunk from the night before... we had been at the casino until five in the morning, and I can remember when the cabby dropped him off out front of his place, how he stumbled and fell forward onto his hands and knees, and we laughed... boy did we laugh. He was always laughing, you see... I guess that's what we do, when everything feels like it's gone sour. What else can you do, really? He said goodnight and I watched him walk on into his apartment building for the last time."

There's a long pause as Jim composes himself while the crowd continues to adjust their positions in awkward anxiety.

"He was my partner in crime. My brother. We fought Al-Qaeda

39

together. We watched our other brothers die. We saw blood pour from the wounds of our friends and enemies alike. And in the end, it was always red. Nothing but red. I still see it... in my dreams. Faucets leaking blood... that soft drip-drip-drip and hallways with holes in the walls..."

"That was my bottom. The day I found Geoff dead in his apartment. Hanging from a pipe in the bathroom. I was still high at this point, hadn't slept from the night before. He used his army issued Teflon rope to do the job... I had two grams of coke on me... and I ended up doing both of them while I waited for the ambo to come... the cops took me into the hospital behind the ambulance... they were alright guys, for cops anyways. I mean they knew I was on something... it had to have been pretty obvious..."

"Anyways..." Jim says, sighing deeply and scratching his temples. "It's been a rough year for me... I guess most of you probably know that already. My wife divorced me in January, and I've been living on my own in a shitty bachelor apartment... my neighbors are older folk, I don't think they like me very much," he pauses. "Everything has been so different since I got back. As most of you know, I was in the Army for ten years, and now that I'm out, I have to say I feel pretty lost. I have a few friends left, but most of them still battle with the addiction, so I don't get to see them much. I don't want to bother them with my own demons – we all have our own battles to fight. It's hard, you know, trying to stay sober when you're all alone. Some nights I wake up in the dark, and I reach out beside me, hoping that her body is still there to keep me warm... but she's not, and the whiskey bottle beside my mattress is the only thing I can reach for. There's something comforting about that burning sensation in my throat, after drinking from the bottle, and I can't help but feel like it's the only friend I have left."

Various people call out from their seats:

"No Jim."

"Hang in there!"

"We're here for you, bud!"

"Thank you," he says, taking a deep breath. "My father passed away around this time last year. He didn't have much, but he was a good man. I used to talk with him every Sunday. He liked to go to church and he would call me after the sermon to tell me about it. It was our routine, you know? I haven't been to church since I was a child, but while my father was still here, when he used to call me on Sundays, I felt like God was still somewhere in my life, like I was still connected, you know? But now I'm not so sure..." he pauses, takes another gulp, "Life is such a mystery to me. There's nothing out there for me except you guys, except for this small podium and these stale cups of coffee, but it helps. I'm not over my addiction yet, but this helps, and I pray that you guys are doing better than me. As most of you know, I have a daughter, Samantha. She has a baby daughter. A beautiful and healthy child... I haven't been allowed to see her yet, but I'm hopeful... I'm so proud of her, and I know that she will talk to me again someday. We haven't spoken in a long time now..."

I shift uncomfortably in my chair while some of the other men sigh. The bearded man sitting in front of me rubs at his eyes because he's crying, the tears getting all caught up in his thick beard. Jim's eyes look glassy, and he gulps and nods, saying; "Well, thank you, that's all for now."

'Way to go buddy.'

'Well said Jim!'

And despite the fact that everyone seemed to admire and look up to my sponsor, I had absolutely no respect for him.

Jim is full of shit. That's the issue.

I know this because the two of us used to go out drinking together after most meetings, back when I first started attending. He was a regular riot, the type of guy who always had a new joke lined up and could chat up nearly anyone in the vicinity of our barstools. But after a certain amount of drinks, Jim's demeanor took on a whole new shade. It always went one of two ways; either he would start blubbering and getting all emotional, or he would try to pick a fight with whichever poor soul happened to look at him the wrong way. The last time we went out together, which was over three months ago, he knocked a man unconscious at the

41

Royal Oak on Kent. I have never seen a man's jaw shift in such an ungodly way, and after the police contacted me the next day, I guess I decided that going out drinking with Jim was probably not the best idea, considering I was forced to lie for him to the cops (and sadly there is no chapter in the AA handbook which outlines proper etiquette for when your sponsor assaults another man while drunk). Thankfully, nothing came of the investigation, but it was an unpleasant source of stress for a couple weeks, and when your structure is as worn and flimsy as mine, any added stress can be a very dangerous thing.

"Is there anyone else who would like to share?" Tony asks the room.

The room stands quiet.

"How about you," Tony says, pointing at me in the back, "I don't believe you've had a chance to share yet, Markus."

"Oh, well – no, thanks. I... can't."

"That's quite alright," Tony says, but I catch Jim looking over in my direction with a furrowed brow.

What in the hell would I have said?

'Hello, my name is Markus.'

'Hi, Markus.'

'My wife is pregnant again, and the last thing I want to do is bring another child into this world, a world that I'm having more and more trouble understanding. My biggest fear is that it will be a girl. Not because she will be vulnerable, quite the opposite. Women are empowered now, it's different than it used to be, and I don't really understand what the modern-day woman is all about. Maybe I'm old fashioned, but with the progression towards more raunchy and sexually explicit material in our society, I fear that my daughter will be a slut. Something about that idea is very intruding and uncomfortable to me, thinking about her being violated like that, and frankly, I'm scared. Ironically enough, I think my son might be gay, which doesn't seem to bother me at all, and I'm actually cheating on my wife with a much younger woman who could be the perfect archetype for the daughter I am so scared of

42

having. My wife writes romance novels which usually end with the female protagonist leaving her husband, oh, and did I mention that our dog is an alcoholic...'

That would be some speech.

"Mark, you need to take this stuff more seriously," Jim tells me on a weekly basis.

And I want to take it seriously! Honestly, I do (despite the religious overtones and terribly clichéd reassurances which permeate the gymnasium on a weekly basis), but the thing is, I can't help but think that no one in here actually gives a shit about the person beside them. Sure, we clap for one another, cheer and call out encouraging things, but in the end, what is it that everyone here seeks? Why do people come here week-in and week-out to profess their failures? Self-vindication.

To be absolved.

It was almost like a confessional at a Catholic church, except rather than being locked in a tiny room with some creepy Priest, we profess our sins and guilt upon one another in a vain attempt to reassure ourselves that, yes, we are really changing for the better. It's not my fault for spending my family's savings on booze and gambling and whores, because this room is full of men and women who have done the same thing, so I must be okay! I must be a goddamn legend for even surviving this long, living with this terrible, debilitating disease.

Yeah, yeah, yeah.

As nice as it would be to blame my actions on some disease, I cannot deny that drinking is a choice I make on my own. It is something that I choose to do, and last time I checked, you can't choose to have a disease, if you know what I mean.

Basically, I thought they were all full of shit, including my sponsor, Jim. I watch him standing up at the front with Tony as the meeting adjourns, shaking hands and hugging the other group members, and I can't help but wonder if he knows just what a self-fulfilling prophecy he is...

You can't count on anyone in this life, that's the one thing I've learned.

And as far as God goes, well Jesus Christ, if you're counting on him to help you, you're already fucked.

I make my way over towards the coffee and doughnuts. Jim comes and stands beside me at the coffee table. His dress shirt is perfectly ironed and tucked into the waist line of his beige pants.

"How are you doing, Markus?"

"Good," I say, "and you?"

"Oh, I'm okay," he says, taking a sip of his coffee and looking around the room. "It's sad to see all of us gathered together like this. It reminds me of a dog pound; a bunch of discarded animals. But it still makes me feel better, to be with all you fellow degenerates."

"Hey, speak for yourself Jimmy Boy, I'm a downright stand-up citizen."

"Ha!" he laughs, "now that's a good one."

A man walking past us squeezes Jim's arm as he passes, and the two of them share a nod. I shift from foot to foot, trying to think of something poignant to say, but Jim's hands are shaking and his face looks like it's been locked in that sort of quasi-frown for some time now.

Jim quickly shoves a bundle of bills into my hand, not wanting to attract the attention of his many disciples.

"That's four hundred there," he whispers in my ear. "I'll have the other six to you next week, hopefully, it's just..."

"No worries," I say, cutting him off before whatever lie he had conjured up this week came spilling from his mouth. "That's fine, Jim."

"Thanks, man. Appreciate it..."

"So, how goes the battle?" he asks after a brief moment of awkward silence, looking up and smiling at me.

"Oh, not bad," I say, suppressing a whiskey drenched burb which threatens to come bombarding from my throat. "I'm winning, I think."

"That's good," he nods. "I guess you are almost done with these little meetings, eh?"

"Yeah, couple more weeks."

"I was hoping that you would keep coming," he says, "even

though you are no longer required. It'd be nice if you finally got up there to share with everyone before you left..."

"Ah, that's going to be tough, Jim. I've got enough going on at home. My wife is pregnant again..."

"Congratulations," Jim says, throwing his arms around me and embracing me. "There's nothing more powerful than having a child."

"Yeah, I guess so."

"It's your chance to make things right."

I nod.

"I have a lot of making up to do with Sam, I'm not sure she can ever forgive me for the things I've put her through..."

"That's... too bad."

"I know she still loves me. It's hard to face sometimes, which is ironic because I end up drinking over it, which is exactly where the goddamn problems all started."

I nod. Circle.

"Have you made it up to your family?"

"Well, I'm not so sure I have anything to make up to them. I mean, it was only a mistake, just the one time..."

"I really wish you would share with the group," Jim sighs.

"I don't really know what I would say, I guess."

"The words will come with time."

I look over towards the round clock hanging above the basketball net, the pointless arms twirling around in a circle while we bounce off one another, desperate to find connection, searching for some sort of hopeless gesture to signify the validity of our existence. My coffee has gone cold and the bitter taste sits all stale upon my tongue. Jim nods his head at me and tells me to take care. I watch him wander off into the crowd and decide it's probably time for me to head home.

When I get home that night, Tracy's friend Natalie is over and the two of them are sitting in the kitchen swooning over the laptop. Natalie is skinny and has pale skin that stretches out tight against her face, making her look ugly and concerned most of the time (except of course when she was gossiping about some other

45

person, in which case her face would light up like a fucking jack-o-lantern). She wears her dark hair up in a bun and applies too much rouge on her cheeks, which have been repeatedly pumped full of Botox, along with her lips. Natalie is a teacher at the same school my wife used to work at. I suppose spending time with Natalie was the only way for her to feel like she was still involved with all of that (otherwise I can't consciously comprehend why Tracy spends time with this woman).

"How was AA?" Trace asks me, all the while Natalie looks at me with a contemptuous coyness that causes my blood to boil.

"It was fine, same as usual. Glad to be almost done with them."

"Hmm," my wife nods. "So that's it, you're done, eh?"

"Hurrah!"

"Are you sure you don't want to keep going?"

"No, I don't think I will, Trace," I say as I make my way to the fridge. "Besides, I can't say it's really done much," I add, emphasizing my point by cracking open a fresh bottle of Budweiser from the fridge.

"What are you two old birds up to?"

"Oh shush, Markus,"

"Yes Markus, shush," Natalie says, "we are updating Trace's Facebook account!"

I cautiously come around the other side of the table to take a look at the computer screen. I can see pictures of a bachelorette party, a bunch of middle aged women drinking out of penis cups with penis straws, meanwhile their wrinkled faces resemble my ball sac. There's nothing more nauseating than a woman pretending to be liberated while they suck from a penis straw. Why don't they try sucking on a real cock for once?

Naturally, Natalie is right smack in the middle of everything, a cardboard party hat perched upon her head, and a giant black penis straw positioned firmly between her lips.

"Dear god..."

"Don't you have Facebook?" Natalie asks, turning to me. Her face gleaming like a porcelain plate.

"No, I don't."

"Well, that's not very fun, is it?"

"I was always under the impression that Facebook is for kids who have a little too much time on their hands."

"You're so old fashioned," Tracy says. "Everyone's got Facebook now."

"That's great," I say, "that's really great. Pretty soon there'll be naked pictures of every man, woman and child up on the fucking internet, at the rate we're going."

"Such a cynic," Natalie says, shaking her head.

"I've got nine friend requests," my wife says, beaming up at me with a smile that sort of breaks my heart. She really was excited about this...

Natalie looks at me with a matter-of-factly face and I wonder when the last time she's had a good lay, it might explain a lot, actually.

"Oh my god!"

"What?" Natalie and I say in unison.

"Thomas declined my friend request!"

"Oh, teenagers – so secretive," Natalie guffaws.

I can only shake my head in disbelieve. Why in the hell would you want to see what your nineteen-year-old son in university is getting up to?

The two of them gawk at each other and blabber on, talking about the various accomplishments and noteworthy moments in their children's lives in a constant game of 1-up; all the while dreaming of the days when their vaginas still looked nice when shaven. I try and block them out while searching the fridge for a beer.

"So, like I was saying Trace," Natalie says, picking up on some irrelevant and lost conversation that must have been going on before I entered the room. "Robert has been going to the gym for three months now, and it's really starting to show. He was getting bigger than he's ever been. I simply told him 'look, there's no way I can keep sleeping with a man who has tits' and you know what? He can flex his pecks now! I've seen him do it in the mirror."

My wife nods, only half listening while she keeps cruising her

Facebook account. It always made me laugh when she referred to her husband as 'Robert' (and she made sure to emphasize the bert). Natalie is the type of woman who only calls men by their full names, even though I've known Bob for about ten years now, and I've never heard anyone else refer to him as anything but Bob.

"It might be a good idea for you to start up a little gym routine, Mark," Natalie says.

God, she was an awful cunt.

"Yes, Markus," my wife chimes in, "a little exercise would be good for you."

"Hmmm," Natalie nods, "and maybe you won't be so afraid to open up a Facebook account when you're a little more... satisfied with the way you look."

My wife nods in distinct approval.

"Thank you, ladies, this has been a very enlightening conversation," I say. "I'm quite satisfied with the way I look, so I'll have to turn down that little gym idea, but I will add, Natalie - if I may - that perhaps you could lay off the old lady perfume next time you're coming over, eh? It smells like my dead grandmother in here."

"Markus!" my wife cries.

"It's okay Tracy," Natalie says. "He knows we're right."

"My friends call me Mark," I say, waving my hand in front of my nose as I retreat to the living room. I hear the two of them laughing from the kitchen, and it makes me wonder what it's like to get away with being such a malevolent and psychotic bitch? Women really do have it made.

When I was twenty, I volunteered in the Member of Parliament for Simcoe-Grey's office on Parliament Hill. His name was Larry Trample, which was fitting, considering he weighed about three-hundred and fifty pounds. He had the swollen, deformed knuckles of an ex-NHLer (hockey players made great Canadian politicians), and we mostly talked about sports, women and barbequing. I learned a lot that year though, more than I ever did in school.

I was going to Carlton at the time, and politics was still something new and exciting to me. I was young and idealistic and did not understand the static nature of the system yet (somehow I still believed that Members of Parliament and my fellow colleagues were all here to make Canada a better place, to enact meaningful and necessary changes based on well thought-out logic rather than blindly regurgitating partisan rhetoric).

I had sex with a thirty-two-year-old woman in the utility room of the Justice Building where everyone did their dishes on the 8th floor. Her name was Candice. She was a tall woman with large breasts and a surprisingly firm ass (for a thirty-two-year-old). I was young and impressionable, which made me a perfect target for such a predatory creature (observe the middle-aged cougar in all the ferociousness and glory of her hunt!). She'd been working in politics for too long, and everything about her was mechanical and efficient (including the sex). She would wink at me as we passed each other in the hallways, her wearing a tightly fitted dress, or perhaps a low-cut blouse with a skirt, and me in my jeans and polo shirt, looking like any other university student. I was never sure why she came on to me, but I never complained. She was just an older woman trying to find her sexuality again. Her husband left her for a younger woman (go figure), and she would often complain to me about the sexual performances of men over thirty.

"They just don't care anymore," she would say, "they don't try hard enough because it doesn't matter to them anymore. All that matters is their bank accounts and their credit ratings, greedy bastards. I haven't had a man go down on me in over five years – do you believe that? Five fucking years of selfishness."

"That is downright criminal."

"You're not scared of a little cunnalingis, are you Marky boy?"

"Not at all, ma'am."

"Let's go do some dishes."

And I would have her spread out on the counter, dirty glasses with stale coffee rattling beside us as I thrusted in and out, trying to be as quiet as possible because there were other offices all around us, and she would bite me on the chest hard, leaving marks and sometimes even bruises. I wasn't a virgin at the time, but I wasn't

49

exactly an expert either, and she would teach me the little things that we learn through practice, like how to tickle her butthole while inside her (she liked it when I stuck my finger in, but I didn't enjoy it much back then – I have no qualms with it now though), or how to arch my cock upwards inside her vagina so that she would cum.

She would come into my office during QP and let me finger her as we sat there on cushioned chairs watching the MPs yell at each other from across the floor of the House of Commons.

"Use two fingers," she would say, "and wiggle them upwards, like a hook, yes, that's it, faster..."

And I would spend time at my desk practicing, forming my middle and index fingers into a hook and wiggling them fiercely in front of my own face. I would practice with my tongue too, because I wanted to be good at all those things, it seemed very important to me at the time, but poor Candice turned out to be right, because now I could give a shit about cunnalingis, or how fast I can move my fingers. To be completely honest, the faster it was over and I got too cum, the better it was. It used to be an art to me; a masterpiece; a production. But over the years of marriage my sex life has become more of a sitcom, the same tired joke over and over and over...

Thursday

My mistress is considerably better looking than my wife, although she is also much younger. I think that my wife would have been able to stand beside her back before Thomas came barging out of her vagina, when she was still young and adventurous and naughty, but now there wasn't much of a competition (my wife doesn't even let me fuck her doggy-style anymore, not that I'd really want to anyways).

Her name is Cheryl and she makes more money than I do working as a lobbyist for Hill and Knowlton. She wears designer clothes, matches her belts with her shoes, and likes to eat at Hy's on weekdays. And I still have no idea why she lets me inside of her. But hey, I'm not complaining! If there's one thing I've learned throughout my younger and more venerable years, it was this; never attempt to understand a woman's motivations.

I met her two years ago at the annual Real Estate Association of Canada gala. A real swanky type event held in the Ball Room of the Chateau Laurier with high ceilings sporting numerous hanging crystal chandeliers, expensive paintings up on the walls, and most importantly, two open bars situated on either side of the room. The event always attracted lots of big-swinging dicks from Parliament Hill, which of course gave the overpaid Government Relations team at the REAC a real sense of accomplishment for which they did not deserve in the slightest (simply place an open bar in any setting, and like animals drawn to water, politicians will surely find their way there).

Cheryl was standing in the corner of the room sipping on a glass of red wine, looking particularly sexy in a tight fitting strapless black dress with matching high-heels, her red lipstick glistening in the dim light, and after consuming one or five double rye and cokes, I approached her in a sudden surge of intoxicated confidence.

"You look bored," I said.

"And you look lost," she responded, smiling.

"Yeah, I left my dick-sucking shoes at home, so, not really sure what I'm supposed to be doing in this room..."

"Drinking," she told me. "You're supposed to be drinking."

"Cheers!"

We clinked glasses and she asked me what I did for a living.

"Ah, another fucking real estate agent, eh?" she said, her eyebrows shifting.

"Sadly, yes. And what is it that brings you into the fray, may I ask?"

"Ah, sadly, I'm another fucking Member of Parliament's wife."

"Oh, I see."

"Yeah, he's standing over there chatting up that group of interns," she said, pointing with her wine glass. "We haven't had sex in six months."

"That's downright unparliamentary!"

"You're telling me."

We exchanged some more words, followed by our phone numbers. She gave me her Hill and Knowlton card and wrote her personal cell on the back, which for some reason turned me on immensely. I called her up the next week and things just sort of fell into place.

We have a pretty usual routine; she will text me sometime in the afternoon, asking if I can fit her in for a quick business meeting. I will almost always respond with an emphatic yes, and I will call up the Minto Suites Hotel, which is located on Lyon Street just a few blocks from my office and has a large lobby with leather chairs scattered around glass-faced tables. She will meet me there and sometimes the two of us will go out for dinner and drinks to dingy pubs where no one will recognize her, but mostly we just fuck in the hotel room and drink there. She wears thongs and push-up bras, and sometimes I make her leave the bra on because it makes her breasts look fantastic.

She is married to Spencer Price, the Member of Parliament for Ottawa - Orleans, the riding in which I happen to reside. I have never met the man, funny enough, despite him being my representative, but through the picture painted by Cheryl, I think it's safe to assume that he is the typical politician, and really, a giant walking cliché (affair with the secretary, penchant for scotch and cigars, you can't make this shit up – it just is).

Cheryl likes it when I hit her during sex. At first it made me pretty uncomfortable and I didn't like wrapping my hands around her throat while I was inside her, but lately it's become something I quite enjoy. She's a very proper woman who dresses in designer clothes, and there's something so satisfying about fucking the proper out of her. She is insatiable, and will sometimes tear the buttons from my dress shirt as she pulls me down on top of her. She often leaves bruises all over my shoulders and chest, and I enjoy coming up with elaborate stories for my wife as to how I acquired them.

Sometimes, in the wake of my guilt and shame, I worry that perhaps my wife is cheating on me, and I will scrutinize her phone and emails, searching through the messages and finding nothing but emails from diet clubs or rejection letters from publishing houses. I guess it was hard for a woman in her position to get out there and meet new people, because people are always looking for certain things; you need to have something to offer. Unfortunately for my wife, there weren't that many adulterers out there who were interested in listening to the plot of her new romance novel, or how her feet are aching because of the pregnancy, or how she enjoys having a cup of coffee every morning on our porch, watching our alcoholic dog mope about the front yard. You see, my wife is a genuinely sweet and nice person, which is why she never made it anywhere in life. She deserves someone infinitely better than me, a man who has compassion and intimacy still coursing through his veins, a man who can see the beauty in children and family and love, but she took a risk and married me, the slick-talking, free-walking, son-of-a-bitch who convinced her that love can last forever.

It breaks my heart that I don't love her anymore.

I'm on my way to the Tim Horton's that's just a few blocks away from my office. The sun is out and the birds are chirping and I suppose I should feel pretty damn good, but there's a slight throbbing in my right testicle and I can feel a nervous sweat break out as I contemplate calling Dr. Von Heyman. Above me, I watch a giant grey cloud come billowing towards the downtown core from the river, all bulbous and puffy, and it reminds me of a cancerous cell, devouring everything in its path.

The sidewalks are crowded as it's close to lunch time and the bureaucrats are bounding past each other, their little ID tags bouncing off their hips. I've yet to meet a bureaucrat who would dream of staying in their office through lunch. Hell, they don't even answer the phone past 3:30pm. The sounds of the city, which used to entice and enthrall me, now disgusted me. The vulgar clattering and obnoxious beeps and horns. It was all symptomatic of our obliviousness.

I can feel the buildings leering down upon me, casting their long shadows like steel giants who mean to clobber me, snuff me out with one foul swoop, and I can't say I'd blame them. I might even thank them in the end.

"Mark!"

Startled, I stop dead in my tracks like a child whose bladder has just come undone. An older woman is walking towards me, a big smile plastered across her wrinkled face. She is wearing bright red lipstick and her hair is a bright reddish colour, clearly dyed. She's wearing a black dress with high heels, and despite her age, I suppose her figure is not that bad. Yet I cannot discern why she looks so familiar, or how in the hell she knows my name.

"Mark," she says again, opening her arms to embrace me.

"Err... do I know you?"

"It's me!" she says, pulling me in for a hug. I can feel the loose flesh hanging from her arms. "Candice, from the Hill."

Dear god. It was. Ol' Candice. I study her face and buried

54

beneath the wrinkles and age spots, I do recognize her. She smiles at me and pats me on the back, then releases me from her grasp. Her breasts feel like soggy potatoes against my chest.

"Don't tell me you've forgotten about our little rendezvous in the Justice Building?"

"Of course not," I smile, forcing my lips to curl upwards with all my might.

"How have you been?" she asks.

"Oh, not too bad. Got a wife and a kid... you know, pretty standard..."

"Mark the married man," she muses. "You know, I still think about that little kitchen..."

"Ah yes," I blush. "It was always fun doing the dishes with you, Candice."

She winks at me and giggles.

"How have you been?" I ask.

"Oh, not bad," she says. "I'm living downtown in a nice one bedroom apartment. I work over at DND, been there for about ten years now."

I take notice of her little ID badge dangling from her hip. Another goddamn bureaucrat. Go figure.

"I got divorced a couple years back," she confides. "Second husband. He was a real asshole. Left me with nothing. It's been sort of a rebuilding the past couple of years."

"That's... unfortunate," I say.

"Yes, it's okay though. I've got my little Sylvester now."

"Sylvester?

"My tabby," she says, as if I should've known about her goddamn cat. "He's absolutely adorable. You should see him. He even plays fetch with me."

And the image of Candice playing fetch with her tabby cat invades my mind like a virus, filling me with an incorrigible sadness that persists throughout the next five minutes of our conversation. She tells me about her first husband, who was a politician and ended up cheating on her with his assistant (surprise, surprise). And I picture Candice lying in bed alone at night, staring up at the

55

ceiling while her cat paws at her feet, and this fills me with a sick sort of dread that I can taste in the back of my throat, because for the first time in a long time, I wonder if perhaps I am taking my life for granted.

"Well, it was swell seeing you Mark," she says, smiling so that the flesh on her cheeks balls up into distorted dimples that look like my dress pants after I've left them sitting in the dryer for too long. "Let me know if you ever need help with the dishes," she adds, winking again.

"You got it, Candice," I say, my feet propelling me in the opposite direction.

And as we both turn away from each other, continuing through the throngs of disconnected individuals, I think to myself; there should be a law prohibiting people over sixty from winking in a sexual manner.

My phone vibrates against my desk, startling me so that I lurch forward in my chair a bit, spilling a couple sheets of paper onto the carpeted floor. I see a text message from Cheryl that says 'business meeting tonight?' I tell her yes and then promptly delete the message. I quickly dial the number for the Minto (I have it memorized), and reserve a single room with one bed. I sit at my desk for twenty more mindless minutes before giving up. I call Trace and let her know I'll be coming home late tonight. She complains about how I'm going to miss dinner (oh no, another goddamn stir-fry!), but I am able to coax her by promising a foot rub when I get home (kill me, please).

On my way to the hotel I stop at the LCBO and buy a 26er of Grey Goose Vodka, and once securely in my room (after a tense moment waiting at the front desk while the concierge ran my credit card through...), I crack the seal and pour myself a stiff Vodka and OJ. The room is horrendously plain and it makes me anxious sitting here on this stiff bed, looking at the beige walls and multi-coloured carpeting that didn't really go with anything else in the room. The lumpy cushioned chair sits lonely in the corner, and I wonder how many depressed and lonely people have spent time sitting in it. Hotels rooms were like hospital waiting rooms. There was nothing permanent about a hotel or a hospital waiting room, you were merely passing through on your way to somewhere else (death?). The perfect purgatory.

My phone vibrates in my pocket and I pull it out, reading the text message; 'what room?'

I finish my drink and promptly pour myself another. It didn't matter how many times I met her here, I was always nervous. I move over towards the bathroom and stand in front of the mirror, looking at my disheveled hair – specs of white beginning to sprout up through the brown. I have some stubble growing in, which also has specs of white and grey in it.

A knock comes on the door.

I slug back my second drink and answer it, holding back a burp in my throat and tasting that black licorice taste in my mouth from the vodka. Cheryl is wearing a white blouse and a high black skirt with heels on, her long brown hair cascading down her left shoulder. She was fashionable and still knew how to be sexy, which was easy for her because she was only thirty-two, still skinny, and had fairly large breasts (plus she'd never given birth to a little monster). She's wearing gold-rimmed glasses which give her a seductive librarian type look.

"Hello there Markus," she says, entering the room swiftly, setting her purse down on the dresser and instantly unbuttoning her blouse at the top, revealing a black lace bra and the luscious tops of her breasts.   "May I have a drink?"

"What's in it for me?" I say.

"Oh, can I interest you in some of this?" she says, undoing another button.

"Coming right up, ma'am."

"Don't call me ma'am, I hate when you call me that."

"Okay, lady-girl."

"That's better," she says, looking down at her open blouse and shrugging, she pulls the entire thing up over her head and collapses on the bed, her flat stomach and bulging chest making me hard. I pour two stiff drinks and approach the bed.

"How is your pregnant wife?"

"She's still pretty pregnant," I say. "She signed up for Facebook..."

"Oh, maybe I'll add her as a friend," she says, winking.

"Be my fucking guest."

"Do you know if it's a boy yet?"

"She hasn't told me. But the baby shower is next week – so at least I have that to look forward to."

"Oh poor Markus," she croons.

"Yes, poor me."

"Let me see here," she says, cupping my balls with her free hand while I stand there beside the bed with a drink in my hand and a massive erection. "Hmm, I can feel them swimming around in there, rambunctious little bastards aren't they? I mean, not every forty-six-year-old can get their forty-five-year-old wife pregnant. They must be strong swimmers, which leads me to believe that it most certainly will be a boy."

"And how is your politician of a husband?" I ask her, while simultaneously grabbing her breasts with my sweaty palms, filling each hand like sweet oranges that haven't quite ripened yet.

"He's still a politician," she says, sighing. "We haven't fucked in three months now."

"What a goddamn travesty."

"You're telling me."

"So, big plans for Easter weekend," I ask, sitting down beside her on the bed and removed my pants.

"Oh god, I've got about five different events I have to attend with Spencer, hanging off his arm like a glorified purse, and then his god-forsaken family is coming over on Sunday, and his mother will undoubtedly criticize the turkey for being too dry, the gravy for being too thick, and this will inevitably lead me to devour an entire bottle of red wine before I say something rude to my mother-in-law, at which point the bitch will finally leave..."

"Wow," I say, shaking my head. "You know, I often wonder why we even bother with these family holidays? I mean honestly, is there a single family out there who actually enjoys this shit?"

58

"Sounds like the starting of a platform," she smiles. "And what will your first act as Prime Minister be?"

"Fucking you in the Speaker's Chair."

"And what do you have planned for the long weekend?"

"Well, my son is coming home tomorrow."

"That's exciting," she says, staring at me intently.

"Yeah, it's real exciting alright. I can't wait to see how much weight he's put on since September..."

"Such a caring father."

"Hey, I care. Of course, I care. I'm not trying to be mean, I just want my son to be healthy..."

"Has he come out of the closet yet?" she asks.

"He says he's not gay, but the jury is still out on that one, in my mind anyways."

"Oh Markus, what would you know about it?" she says, smiling mischievously up at me, the rapid rise and fall of her breasts causing me to lose focus.

I reach out my hand and grab her around the throat. She licks her lips and tosses back her drink in one giant gulp. I set mine down on the side table and leap on top of her, pinning her down and ripping her skirt off, revealing a set of beautifully smooth legs, a black thong and just a hint of pubis. I slap Cheryl in the face hard and then go down on her, shoving my face recklessly into her wonderful cunt, lapping like a dog laps for water as she pulls my hair and scratches at my shoulders with her fingernails. I climb back up on top of her and stick my tongue down her throat violently, grabbing her light brown hair in a fist and yanking on it. I can feel her fingernails digging into my back and the burning ache excites me. I bite her neck, pick her up and slam her down on the bed, removing her bra in one swift move with my well trained fingers, unclipping the back and then attacking her breasts, licking her nipples and sucking on them, 'bite them,' she whispers, 'bite them harder,' and my fingers wander down south, her pussy is wet and I can't bear to wait any longer, thrusting inside her roughly with my hard cock, and she bites my chest so hard that a bruise instantly appears all red and purple above my left nipple. 'Choke me,' she says, then screaming; 'CHOKE ME!' I hoist her out from under me and flip her around onto her stomach, spreading her legs while simultaneously wrapping my arm around her throat in a chokehold. I watch her eyes flutter and I keep fucking her until finally we both cum and I can let go. And after it's all over, both of us lying in a heap, sweaty and exhausted, bruised and sore, she rubs the hair on my chest and I wrap my arm around her waist, pulling her close so that I can feel her soft breath against my neck, and she tells me how she's afraid she'll die alone.

Friday

Good Friday. Praise Jesus! Apprehension hangs in the air as I contemplate exactly just how much weight my son has put on since I last saw him (and a sinister after thought: how many times has he had sex? And was this hypothetical sex with a hypothetical man or woman?). After first semester, he came home with an extra chin, and a sense of self-entitlement that only university can bestow upon a young man. Thomas flat out denied that he was a homosexual when I accidentally asked him that last time he was home (and no, my inadvertent question did not help to improve our already tattered relationship). Still, I don't believe him.

Trace is busy about the house, putting up Easter decorations throughout the living room and kitchen. Flowers, fake birds, died eggs (which she stayed up late last night making), little straw baskets set delicately by the fireplace containing tiny stuffed bunnies. It really was enough to make you sick. What did bunnies and eggs have to do with Easter anyways? Why don't we stick to the traditions, huh? Why not gouge some holes in me and see if I wake up on Sunday? Just drape me over the couch and stick some goddamn rye whiskey in my hand, and I assure you, I'll come back to life. Give me my crown of thorns; just make sure there's some Crown Royal too.

The living room window is open and the sun is high in the sky this afternoon, beaming in through the window and casting a glare on the television. The birds tweeting in the sky fill me with a sort of listless anxiety. What did they have to be so fucking chipper about? It is unseasonably hot out, giving me fantasies of patios with short-skirted waitresses and Caesars and frothing pints of golden beer.

You have a problem.

Yeah, well you certainly don't help things none, Mr. High and Mighty.

You realize I'm you, right?

Shut-up.

"Markus! Can you please cut the lawn?" Trace hollers at me from upstairs, where she is rummaging around looking for more redundant decorations. How many stuffed bunnies did we own, for Chrissakes?

I take a peek out the living room window and see that our grass is for the most part yellow and dead. I think about expressing this sentiment to my wife, however, deep down I know it will make no difference. When Trace was in her company-is-coming mode, it was an exercise in futility to attempt reasoning with her, and would only induce potential temper tantrums and stress induced explosions.

"I don't think we have any gas..." I say in a vain attempt to forgo any immediate excursion of physical activity.

"I picked some up yesterday, sweetheart."

"Oh, great. Thanks... hunny."

What a bitch.

I hear her come bounding down the stairs, arms full of more colourful Easter shit, and part of me hopes she slips halfway down, maybe crack her head off the railing and come tumbling to the bottom in a tornado of fluorescent reds, oranges and greens. But then the image of her paralyzed in a wheelchair crops up into my mind and I am instantly horrified and start praying that she makes it down safely without breaking her spine, because let's be honest here, there's nothing more terrifying than having a drooling cripple for a spouse.

My cell phone comes to life in my pocket, startling me so that an uncomfortable jolt of what I suppose is energy goes rushing up my spine.

"Markus speaking."

"Hello Mark, it's Josh and Linda here."

Oh, how I loved it when couples called in together over

speakerphone. I suppose if a man is ever looking to gage just how much of his manhood was contained in his wife's purse, the duel call was a great marker for complete and utter surrender. Mr. and Mrs. Josh and Linda Scholace, although their name might as well be Clueless, seeing as it's been well over a year now and after showing the engaging couple over fifty different homes in pretty much every goddamn neighborhood in Ottawa and the surrounding regions, they have yet to come close to making a purchase. They were just about the most boring, indecisive people I had ever met.

"Hello you two, what a nice surprise to hear from you on this beautiful long weekend..."

"You're welcome," they say in unison, oblivious.

"So, what can I help you with?"

"We were hoping we could attend a couple showings this weekend with you."

"Um, you guys do realize it's Easter, right?"

"We're Jewish," they say, again in unison. It's like talking to a couple of synchronized robots.

"Ah, yes. Well, I'm not so sure. My son is coming home for the holidays and my wife would certainly be upset if I absconded all afternoon tomorrow..."

"That's very unfortunate to hear," Linda says.

"Yes," Josh adds, "very unfortunate."

I pause, not knowing what to say.

"I suppose we could call another Realtor, one who is free this weekend..."

Fuckers.

"My friend Arnie is probably available," Joshua says hopefully.

"Now, now," I pipe in. "No need to call Arnie, or Ishmael, or any other Realtor. How about we meet for 11am tomorrow at my office?"

Trace is now standing over me, waving her arms in my face and mouthing the word no over and over again. It was just about the worst mime act you've ever seen.

"Saturday doesn't work for us, unfortunately," Mrs. Scholace says.

"Sabbath," Joshua adds.

"Okay, okay, how about Sunday?"

Pause. What sort of sick game were these turds playing? Were they not the ones insisting that this had to happen this weekend?

"Okay Mark, we appreciate it."

"Yes, Mark, we really do appreciate it."

At this point I can no longer decipher which one of them is speaking. I say no problem and hang up.

"What was that all about?" Trace asks, her arms crossed.

"Jews don't celebrate Easter, apparently."

"So what? You're working Sunday now? Jesus Mark, you'll be gone all afternoon."

"I'll be quick. These two don't have a clue what they want and I'm not planning on wasting too much time on them."

Tracey sighs and I prepare myself for the onslaught of guilt ridden passive aggressive comments, but they don't come. Instead, to my horror, she smiles. "Well I suppose that's okay. We have the whole week to spend with Thomas."

"What do you mean the whole week?" I say in panic, leaning forward in my seat.

"It's his reading week, Markus. He told us that a month ago. He's coming home for the weekend and staying the entire week after!"

"Oh... hurray."

"You could sound more excited."

"I am excited baby. I'm thrilled."

"Good," she says, smiling again. "Now, get off your ass and go cut the grass."

It's 4:02 pm and I'm on my fourth rum and coke when I hear my wife making noises. Half the time she sounded like an exotic bird to me. Her shrill voice cracking in that high-pitched way that makes me wonder if she is simply a fourteen-year-old girl trapped within the body of a forty-five-year-old woman. She rushes past me on the couch and I can see that her baby bulge has grown substantially in the past week. Fabulous. The fucking miracle of life.

64

Somehow, I'm beginning to think that death may be the real miracle.

Please don't be a girl, please don't be a girl...

"Markus! Get up off your ass and come see our son."

I stand with all the alacrity of a convict approaching the stand, grunting in a way that even I find quite displeasing. I hear a car door slam as I make my way towards the foyer. I watch my wife fling open the front door and go running down our pathway, arms raised in the air, making more noises.

"Oh my goodness, Thomas, look at you!"

Dear lord, how many pounds did my poor, lethargic son pack on?

I make my way to the front door and stand in utter shock and apprehension. The tall, gangly kid hugging Tracey cannot be my son. There is no flab hanging from his underarms, no love handles overflowing from the sides of his hoodie, his gaunt face and sunken eye-sockets, no second or third chin, and the fact that I can actually decipher his jaw-line fills me with a sort of jealous happiness that I cannot quite control or understand. He looks... good. And for some reason, this leaves me feeling uneasy.

My wife finally releases her grip on our son and he begins moving his way towards me. I notice that he now has a piercing above his left eye (which side was the gay one again?), and I see the tiny piece of jewelry glinting in the sun as he comes closer.

"Thomas," I say, reaching out my hand.

He hesitates before giving me the limpest, dead-fish handshake I've ever felt. Goddamnit. Is this the man I created? Was this the best I could do? He gives me a meagre smile and nod, moving past me with about as much interest as you might walk past a poster on a telephone pole. You inconsiderate, ungrateful, little piece of subhuman shit...

Calm yourself, Markus. Have another drink for Chrissakes.

Good idea.

I was being facetious.

Thomas ascends the stairs two at a time and I take notice of just how skinny his legs have become. I can see the outline of muscles in his calves and there is a slope in his lower back that seems foreign and completely alien to me.

For a fleeting moment, I wonder if this person is actually my son. If maybe he hadn't been abducted and replaced by a species of saucer-flying aliens who are currently prodding and experimenting on my still overweight and most likely homosexual son.

Then I pour myself another drink, resuming my position on the couch to watch the Jays game, and as so many modern-day men before me, I attempt to bury my own self-reservations and worries by over emphasizing just how much I actually care about sports. Go Jays! Come on, Donaldson, step it up. Our pitching is just garbage. Really need to work on that bullpen. It's shameful. And don't get me started about Dickey...

So many useless words. But still, it makes me feel better.

I can hear my son rustling around upstairs in his room, and I suddenly feel unwanted in my own goddamn house. I feel as if I am trespassing, interfering and am overall a nuisance.

I'm not a racist, but sometimes I fucking hate immigrants.

Every morning, as I go through my banal machinations and rituals, stopping at Timmy's for my cardboard cup filled with brownish water that almost tastes like coffee, I am confronted with an Asian person of small stature behind the counter, who proceeds to repeat my order, incorrectly, three goddamn times before eventually I get a cup of hot chocolate, at which point I am forced to start raising my voice and pointing aggressively with my maniacal fingers.

As I said, I'm not racist. I am a product of the Western society's liberal agenda. A baby-boomer who was brought up to believe that all humans were created equal and that all religions should be celebrated and cherished. Funny enough, we were waging race wars and holy wars all throughout the 50s, 60s, 70s, 80s, did I mention the 90s? Oh, and don't even get me started about the various new sorts of wars we've created in the new millennium.

Muslims and Terrorists and Communists, oh my!

The hypocrisy of it all, of course, and the irony, is that now, I can't even say Merry Fucking Christmas without some towelhead liberal throwing their arms up in the air, lamenting to Allah or Mohammad, or whoever the fuck they pretend exists up there, meanwhile, they demand to have prayer sessions in school and refuse to let women show their faces in public. I mean, whatever, I'm a jealous bastard too, but what's the point of having a woman if you can't show her off a bit? Unless of course they all have faces like horses, which I suppose would explain the whole face scarf thing...

Okay, I know I'm falling off the racially unbiased tracks here, so to speak...

But seriously, I'm not racist. I just find it completely fucking back-ass-wards that the extreme left seems so stubbornly intent on defending a culture which is for lack of a better word, notoriously misogynistic. Do they realize they are betraying the very foundations of their ideology by supporting this shit?

But seriously, I'm not racist.

Let me put it this way. I read an article in the Toronto Star last week (and yes, I know it's my own damn fault for reading that shameless liberal rag), and this article described the plight of a young Punjabi man who was accosted by police and forced to remove his turban. Now, the fella was driving drunk on the 401 and blew double what I did when I got my DUI, but because the cops forced him to remove his turban, this guy gets off scot-free. No DUI. No reckless driving charge. No thousands of dollars extra each year on his insurance. In fact, the goddamn police were forced to apologize to him! Where's my fucking apology, huh?

I guess that's what I'm trying to say... but seriously, I'm not racist!

My supposedly gay son, whose generation is so liberally brainwashed that he doesn't seem to notice race at all (which I find ignorant in its own special, liberal, sort of way), finds my views shocking and bigoted. He is often times ashamed of me, so I guess those feelings are mutual between us.

"Dad, you can't say that!"

"Can't say what?"

"You can't generalize an entire culture. That's what Republicans in America do."

"I didn't say he was a terrorist. I just said he looks like a terrorist."

"Not all Muslims are terrorists, dad."

"Yes, but all terrorists are Muslim."

"That's not true either," my son sighs, looking at me as if I'm some sort of house pet that just shit on the floor. "What about Timothy McVeigh? Or Charles Manson? Or any other of the many Caucasian terrorists who have been the perpetrators of destruction and mass murder in North America? What about the IRA? Or the ETA in Spain? There are terrorists everywhere, dad. Only recently have we started correlating terrorism with Muslims."

Yea, thanks for the history lesson. Sometimes I wonder if my son thinks he is the first person to ever crack open a text book.

The last time I saw my son, he called me reductive. I had to google what it meant: tending to present a subject or problem in a simplified form, especially one viewed as crude.

I can't really argue with that assessment, but I will say that I find it arbitrary and unfair. Sometimes problems are simple. It's human nature to compound these things, to add layers when really there's only one goddamn level.

What these liberal turds don't understand is that they need bitter old bastards like me. They need my bone-headed stubbornness to keep our goddamn culture intact. Without guys like me, we'd all be wearing hijabs and niqabs by the end of the century. Maybe before.

Saturday

It's Saturday and after running over to Westboro to do an Open House, I return home to find my now skinny son lounging on our living room couch. The piercing in his eyebrow greets me with a wink, the fake diamond glinting in the sunlight shining through the window.

"Markus!" Trace calls from upstairs. "Why don't you take Thomas out for lunch?"

Thomas stirs from his TV inspired hypnosis and gives me a look similar to how a person who just realized they drank a mouthful of expired milk might react.

"Trace, he doesn't want to go out for lunch!"

"Thomas! Don't you want to go out for lunch with your father?"

"Sure," he hollers back, looking at me again and shrugging.

"Okay then," I say. "Let's do it."

"I have to get ready first," Thomas says, rising from the couch.

"You're just having lunch with your old man, what is there to get ready for?"

Thomas rolls his eyes at me and bounds up the stairs.

I liked you better when you were a fat-assed teenager who only wore stretched out t-shirts and didn't have a goddamn piercing in your eyebrow, or gel in your hair.

What in the hell were they teaching kids these days at university? (Other than promiscuity, entitlement, and alcoholism, of course.)

I've never really seen eye to eye with my ultra-liberally minded son. He was admittedly much smarter than me in many ways. He just lacked a realistic view point. His ideas (which resembled my own when I was his age, as much as I hate to confess), were not

69

based in reality. They were based in a fantasy world were humans acted out of compassion rather than greed.

I spent eighteen years trying to teach him this simple fact. Our debates have always been highly contentious. Ever since he turned sixteen, I saw the anti-establishment syndrome rise drastically inside of him like an out of control flame.

"Did you know," he used to turn to me while we were driving somewhere, just the two of us alone (he always liked to ambush me with these sorts of questions), "that Henry Ford sold cars to the Nazis?"

"Well, no..." I would respond, reeling as I scrambled to find a way to trump his inevitable point.

"Yeah, not just cars either. War Vehicles. So did GM Motors, and General Electric. They all sold things to the Nazis, and made money from the war. And then, after the war was over, they sued the Allied Forces for bombing their factories in Europe. Do you believe that?"

"Well," I shrug, "pretty smart move, really."

"Dad! How can you say that?"

"Fuck, I don't know, son. I mean its capitalism, you know? It's savage. It's greed. But you know what, it's better than all the rest. Than the alternative... You think you'd be wearing those Nike shoes if it wasn't for Henry Ford?"

"That's not the point, dad."

"What is the point, then?"

"We... You... they made cars for the Nazis!"

"And they made cars for us, too."

"That's the point right there, it's not right," he would cry, slamming his fists in the air. "We're no better than the Nazis. We're the same."

"No son," I would say with a smile. "We are not the same. We won."

And my chilling revelation based in the most opaque and unforgiving of realities would always stifle him, causing his face to turn red as he sat there with his pudgy arms crossed across his flabby chest. My son the social rights leader. God help me.

After forty minutes my son finally descends the stairs, looking pretty much exactly the same as he did when he left the couch.

"You look fabulous," I tell him.

"I know," he says.

We sit in silence as we drive down towards the Market. The traffic is all start and stop, as per usual. I turn up the radio and let myself escape in an old Bruce Springsteen song. After a minute, my son reaches out and turns down the volume. I give him an icy glare that he seems impervious to, and after a few seconds I reach out and turn the volume up again.

"Why do you have to listen to it so loudly?"

"I thought you were a university student? You guys are supposed to like loud music."

Thomas shrugs, looking out the window completely disinterested. Fucking generation Y or Z or whatever they were called, always so nonchalant, always so disinterested. In this world of superficial customized bliss, why bother listening to anyone else's opinion or worries? If I'm not following you on Twitter, then clearly, I don't give a shit about what you have to say.

We get to the Market and by some miraculous chord of luck I find an open parking space on York Street. We stroll into the Heart and Crown for some good old fashioned Irish-styled Canadian pub-food, which amounted to over-sized burgers, under cooked fries, and a whole lot of deep-fried shit. God bless culture. The bar is styled in the typical old-Irish way, lots of dark hardwood and Guniess posters up on the walls. We get a booth table at the back of the restaurant and I try not to stare at our waitress's tits while my son watches, which takes considerable effort considering that her low-cut top is pretty much barfing the tops of her tits out into the wide-open world.

I order a beer and Thomas asks for warm water with lemon slices. More and more I am starting to believe that I would be having a much better time at university than my son.

"Why not get a beer? Jesus Christ son, I'm the one who should be ordering lemon water."

"Beer has too many cals," he says, shrugging again and looking down to study the laminated menu.

"I liked you better when you didn't give a shit about calories."

"Did you? Is that why you always called me tubby and thought I was gay?"

"Well, I thought you were gay because of your penchant for cover-up and techno music and, well... you did dress up in your mother's pantyhose that one time..."

"I was five."

"Still..."

My son sighs.

The waitress comes back with our drinks and asks for our food orders. I get a burger with fries while my now vegetarian son orders a Greek Wrap minus the chicken with a side garden salad. I stare at him in disbelief, but he's too busy typing away on his iPhone to even notice. Ten minutes go by without him looking up once. I sip at my beer and make strange noises with my throat, gradually rising in volume just to see how much it really takes to draw my son's attention away from his cell phone. I don't know a goddamn thing about him, I realize suddenly, and I don't have the slightest idea where to start. Finally, I just blurt out the word FUCK and finally, my beloved son looks up from the tiny screen, giving me a quizzical look.

"What?" he asks.

"Fuck, this is one tasty beer."

That awkward fog of silence returns, settling over us like a warm blanket. I stare at my son from across the table and watch him attempt to look at everything in the goddamn room except for me, his neck twisting and craning about like a goddamn seagull. Our attention spans have evaporated in the wake of mass customization and cell phones, and it was challenging to keep anyone's devoted attention for more than five minutes, unless of course you happened to be a cell phone or a computer.

"Dad, I've been meaning to ask you something..."

Here it comes. "What's that son?"

"Well, it's about someone I met... at school."

He's finally doing it. He's coming out. Hallelujah!

"Whatever it is, Thomas, you can tell me."

"I've met someone, she's amazing - really smart, pretty smile, amazing eyes...."

She? Fuck. Did he say she?

"...and I was wondering if it would be alright if she came to our house for Easter dinner?"

I am still too stunned to speak; staring down at my glass as if the beer had just started speaking. I still can't believe it. Why couldn't he be gay? I mean, yeah sure, he tried to convince me that he wasn't. But I honestly never believed him.

"What's her name?" I ask, not really giving a damn what her name is, but it's the only thing I can think to say.

"A'ishah. She's from Syria."

"Ah, of course... of course she is."

"What, dad?" my son says, leaning forward in his seat and glaring at me with eyes that say my father is an old bigoted white man.

"Um, won't she be a bit put-off with the whole, you know, Jesus thing?"

"Don't be so close minded, dad. Easter isn't just about Jesus. It's about family and connecting and sharing."

I shrug, because it's all I can think to do.

"Do you have something against Muslims?"

"You mean, besides their intense belief in a false deity?"

"Dad!"

"Son, I don't hate the Muslims any more than I hate the Catholics or the Mormons or the goddamn Satanists - they're all the same to me. Foolish. I don't respect foolish people."

"Just because they don't see things your way, they're foolish, eh? What if you're the fool, dad?"

"Do you believe in God?" I ask him.

"Of course not."

"Well then what are you yelling at me for?"

"I may not believe in God, but I do believe in a person's right to believe in whatever they choose."

"Even if that belief causes people to kill each other?"

"It's the government that makes people kill each other."

"Who do you think controls the goddamn Religions?"

At this point I realize that I'm yelling and everyone in the goddamn restaurant is staring at us with slanted eyes. My son is steaming, arms crossed and breathing heavily across from me, his salad turning brown in front of him as I attempt to restrain myself from continuing to berate him.

"So, can she come?" he asks again in defiance.

"Of course she can come," I say, unable to flinch in this morality game of chicken that my son and I have now become engaged in.

"You sure you don't have a problem with that, dad?"

"So long as she doesn't wear one of those goddamn things over her face..."

"Dad, it's called a niqab."

I stare at him in disbelief.

"So..."

"Yes, she does occasionally wear a niqab."

"Excellent," I say, reaching for my beer. "I can't wait to meet her."

He rolls his eyes at me for the second time within an hour and I'm about to give him a piece of my mind regarding his constant rolling of eyes and shrugging of shoulders, but then our food arrives and I decide to just fill my mouth with calories. Throughout the rest of our meal we exchange a total of ten words, and then I pay the goddamn bill and we leave. Part of me wonders if other people around our table can sense the awkward vibes emanating from us like radioactive pulses. I truly know nothing about my son, and the more I try to get to know him, the less I want to know. I suppose he probably feels the same about me.

In the car, I leave the radio off and speed home as fast as I can so as to avoid any further awkward contact with my alien son. Tracy smiles when we get home and asks us both how lunch was?

"Great," we say in unison, and then my son rushes upstairs and I hear the door to his room slam shut. Great.

That night I come stumbling down the stairs around 3am (this is after consuming nearly an entire bottle of spiced rum), for a little midnight snack. I take notice of Maximus lying all sprawled out at the bottom of the stairs, taking care to step over his furry golden mass. Little fucker. I really did love him, despite all the neglect. He was the only one who got me. He was a drinker.

I find some cooked pasta in the fridge and begin wolfing it down without bothering to heat it up. Oh, the luxurious life of a middle-aged alcoholic.

On my return trip towards the stairs, walking crookedly with my arms wrapped around my torso like an elderly homeless woman in winter, I look at our passed-out dog lying contently on the hardwood floor, and before I can really notice that the usual rise and fall of his body is absent, my feet are suddenly slipping out from beneath me, and suddenly the air is all horizontal and my arms flail out in a helpless attempt to catch myself. The hardwood floor comes up to greet me with a great smack, leaving me windless as I roll from side to side in piss and shit.

"You littler fucker!" I croak, pushing Maximus, attempting to wake him.

But the dog doesn't move.

"Maximus! Bad dog!"

Still nothing.

I hear Tracey from above come storming out from our room, flicking on the lights in the upstairs hallway. She is yelling at me, I'm quite sure of it, although I can't actually hear her, because it's at this point that I realize Maximus is dead, and my head fills with a sour ringing as I attempt to rise from my dead dog's piss and excrement. How could he do this to me? You selfish bastard, Maximus.

I see my son has now entered the fray, standing with Trace at the top of the stairs, both of them staring down at me in horror, all wide eyed and gawking, and before I can understand it or control it, I burst into a sobbing laughter, a wretched and offensive sounding cackle that makes my wife and son cringe, because it has just dawned on me, now that Maximus is dead, I am the biggest alcoholic in the house.

Sunday

Mr. and Mrs. Scholace give me a disgruntled look as my phone begins to ring in my pocket. I pull out my cell and see that it's Trace calling. We are standing out front of a wide Victorian house in Orleans that is situated in a gated community where the front lawns are long and narrow and the houses are separated by about a pencil's length. The sun is high in the sky and I can see a hawk flying overhead, probably sensing my impending death and waiting for the chance to bite into my decaying flesh.

"Pardon me," I tell them, and I watch Linda share a look with her husband that says, how dare he? I make sure to walk a good distance away from my charming clients as I'm sure this conversation will be anything but pleasant.

"Hello sweetie," I say in my softest voice.

"I still can't believe he's gone," she sobs into the phone. "It's not the same here without him."

"I know."

"I've decided that we are going to bury Maximus in the back yard. Can you pick up a new shovel on your way home?"

"Can't we just put him in a bag at the end the driveway, Trace? I mean, it's not like he'll know the difference..."

"Markus!"

"Okay, okay, I'll pick up a damn shovel."

"The baby is kicking lots today," she says in a lovey-dovey voice.

"Splendid."

"You should be more excited!"

"I am excited!"

"No you're not," she pouts.

"Baby, I'm about as fucking excited as a man can be when he's dealing with a dead dog and a forty-five-year-old wife who's seven months pregnant!"

I can hear her muffled sobs on the other end of the line, and this only infuriates me further. How am I supposed to keep up with these drastic mood swings? In case you haven't noticed, I'm not exactly the pillar of emotional stability, and dealing with this constant back and forth was surely leading me to an early grave. At least I'll finally get some peace and quiet down there in the dirt.

"I'm sorry, Trace," I say, the words almost choking me. "I'll try to get off early. And I can't wait to feel your belly and say hi to our little man..."

"Oh Markus," she says, coming around. "We don't know if it's a little man or a little woman."

"Well, the universe owes me one," I say.

"Good-bye, my love."

"Yes, good-bye babe."

And finally, she hangs up.

I return to my oh-so-hard-done-by clients who are currently standing and frowning at the corner of the house.

"So, what do you guys think of the place? Great neighborhood, very affordable, and there's plenty of room on the property for add-ons if that's what you were thinking..."

"That looks like mold," Mr. Scholace says, pointing up towards the corner of the roof. He's wearing a buttoned shirt that is far too tight around the belly, his beige khakis hiked up well past his waistline.

"That's concerning," Mrs. Scholace adds. She is wearing a frilly summer dress with hideous white nylons on her pork-chop-like legs.

I crane my neck and attempt to find the spot of concern. Tucked in the corner of the roof where the two walls meet is a palm-sized patch of blackness which could be anything from spider webs, mud, or even black paint... but certainly not mold.

"This house has been assessed and cleared," I tell them, doing everything within my power to keep the smile upon my face from transforming into a straight-lined grimace. I can literally feel my blood pressure rising as my face begins to boil, that sort of tingling in your arms that signifies you might be on the verge of a killing rampage. Either that or a stroke.

"Well," Josh says, looking at me above his gold-rimmed glasses. "When was this assessment conducted exactly?"

"Five months ago."

The two of them exchange a worried glance and I can see it coming before Linda opens her lip-stick stained mouth.

"I think we'll have to pass on this one," she says. "It just doesn't seem to be the one, you know?"

"Oh, I know..." I say, grinding my teeth. "But you haven't even seen the inside yet..."

"Do you have any other houses you can show us today?"

"Oh sure," I say, waving my hand. "There's two more I've got lined up."

And as we walk towards our cars, I suppose I should be annoyed that the Scholaces are keeping me busy all afternoon on a wild fucking goose chase for the immaculate house that lays golden eggs, or whatever the fuck it is they are looking for, and normally I would be pissed off, but since their indecisiveness is effectively keeping me away from home (where my son is, and where my mother-in-law is soon to be), I cannot really complain, and I listen to the radio loudly as I drive onwards to our next destination, singing along with the Barenaked Ladies and trying to forget the fact that if I don't sell a home within the next month, I will probably lose my own.

If I had a million dollars...

I walk in through the front door, shovel in hand, at 4:45pm. I am careful not to swing the door open too quickly... and then I remember that Maximus is dead and so I don't have to worry about hitting him with it. I guess that sort of makes me sad for the first time, and I take a moment to pause in the front hallway. My moment of serenity is spoiled by the fact that Trace has evidently been putting up more decorations over the course of the day, and our entire house looks like Tinkerbelle vomited all over it.

"Honey, is that you?"

"Yes, my dear," I answer, kicking off my shoes.

"Did you get the shovel?"

"Yes, I got the shovel."

"I can't believe he's gone!" she laments, throwing her arms in the air. Women. You had to hand it to them; they were masters of the overly dramatic.

"He's in a better place now," I say, walking over to her and placing a hand on her lower back.

She smiles and looks up at me and I can see some of her sadness melt away.

"I'll start digging."

"Can you take the garbage out too, sweetie?"

"Jesus Fucking Christ! Can't the boy get off his ass to do something?"

"Markus!"

"Fine, fine."

I take the garbage out to the garage, being careful not to step upon the lumpy tarp in the center of the cement floor. Fittingly enough, there are a couple boxes of empty two-fours sitting beside him, which I can only assume Maximus would approve of. Poor little bastard. I exit the garage quickly before the stale smell of death can permeate my nostrils.

I grab the shovel from inside and step out into my backyard from the sliding kitchen door. The fresh air feels good in my lungs as the sun begins its descent in the spring sky, all orange and ominous. It wasn't a bad little backyard, as far as backyards in Orleans go. It was a good fifteen feet wide and stretched all the way back until the wooded area.

The April ground is cold and wet. It takes me a half hour of solid digging before the hole goes deep enough. My shoulders and forearms ache, and I feel a stab of pain in my lower back when I stand up straight. I can feel a blister on the index finger of my right hand. One more gift from my dead dog.

I throw down the shovel and stare into the hole. A cold hard hole in the ground; the best a man (or dog) could hope for. He's in a better place now. Oh, the bitter-sweet irony. Since when did soil and worms constitute a better place? What did that say about the world we live in, eh? I guess damp soil and hungry worms were an arguably better option than reality TV shows and hashtags.

Leaning on the shovel, I study my backyard in all its suburban glory. Tall wooden fences along the sides to separate my yard from the neighbours', with an opening at the back that leads out into the wooded area behind our house. There's a path through the trees that leads down to a park, and I used to take Maximus and Tommy there, when all three of us were much younger and life didn't seem so dismal. Before the worms and soil. And the three of us would walk down the path to the park and I'd have a football or a soccer ball or any kind of ball and Thomas and I would throw it back and forth while Maximus chased between us.

The sun is setting and the dull orange glow in the sky creates a sort of picturesque scene. A man stands in his backyard beside a freshly dug grave, the sun setting below the treetops as a nameless neighbour behind a wooden fence steps out back to have a cigarette. His eyes reach just above the top of the fence, and he nods at me as our eyes meet. It strikes me then that I've never so much as asked this guy how his day is going, let alone learned his name or mowed his lawn while he was away on vacation. Did neighbours still do those types of things? It's hard to say.

"Is that hole there for Maximus?"

I'm so startled by his voice that I jump a bit and whirl around. My nameless neighbour has walked up to the fence and is peering over at me, smoke billowing above his head as the wind catches it and carries the silver fog off into the sky. Apparently, I was not nameless to him.

"Err, yes it is," I say.

"So sad to see him gone."

"Yeah, it really is."

After a few moments of silence, the man says goodnight and I watch him flick his cigarette butt towards the woods. A cool spring breeze sends a shiver down my spine.

I start heading towards the house, wincing at the sharp pain in my lower back. My wife meets me at the door. "Is it ready?" she asks, her face set with a grim sort of urgency that makes me want to laugh out loud (LOL!).

"Yes," I nod, trying to match her serious demeanor.

"Okay, I'll go get Thomas."

I nod and move past her, eager to get this dreadful little funeral over with.

I enter the garage and stand over the tarp containing my dead dog. I can't stand looking at his unmoving silhouette hidden beneath the sheet my wife has thrown over him, and so I pull the sheet off and look into Maximus's eyes one last time, the poor bastard. His dead eyes are like black marbles. I decide to throw the sheet back on top of him.

"Good-bye old buddy," I say out loud as I carry him from the garage, taking the long way around so as not to walk him through the house. "I'll have a couple mix drinks for you to..."

And then it hits me.

The tears stream down my cheeks in wet-hot rivers of shame and regret. I hope he had a good life. I hope he was happy. And I can't help but think that my partner in crime has now vanished. My one and only confidant in this household of creatures bent on destroying me. By the time I've made it around back, I'm full on bawling and I can see my son staring at me with a confused and embarrassed look on his face.

"Oh Markus!" my wife cries as I set Maximus down in the cold hard hole. "Don't worry my love, you still have us!"

Yes, and that's exactly why I'm fucking crying.

After I finish burying Maximus, the tears now dry and dead upon my cheeks, I come in through our back door. I can hear Trace banging around in the kitchen, the scent of half-cooked turkey wafting through the damp air. She always gets so stressed whenever her mother comes over. I often wondered why she even bothered inviting her, because it certainly didn't seem to bring any sort of

81

joy or happiness to either of their lives. It could have something to do with the fact that Tracey's mother is an inconsolable and judgmental bitch, or maybe that my wife is an insecure panic-prone woman with little self-confidence... or wait, maybe the one is a product of the other... fuck it, who cares?

We used to have to put Maximus out in the garage since Tracy's mother hates dogs and is also blind. She has macular degeneration as well as glaucoma, and despite my suggestions of acquiring some medical marijuana, she continues to be a cold-hearted and bitter old hag, claiming that weed is for blacks and hippies. She carries a long wooden stick with her everywhere, like some sort of lifeless pet. It's remarkable, but somehow she is able to whack me across the shins with incredible accuracy every time I try to sneak past her, despite her complete lack of vision.

"Can I get a little help in here!" Tracy cries.

"Yeah, okay, here I come," I say, looking over at Thomas to see if his mother's cry for help has resonated any sort of motivation to move him from the couch where he is currently all sprawled out with his phone held up about five inches from his face, typing frantically into the key pad with his now long and skinny fingers. I'm still not convinced he isn't an alien intruder, and my eyes linger on him a little too long so that he notices and looks at me with narrowed eyes and asks, "What?"

"Nothing," I say, shuffling away.

I enter the kitchen before my wife can throw another hormone induced hissy-fit, and I go over to the stove where the water is already boiling and start plopping the potatoes into the pot, trying my damnedest to look earnest. The kitchen is a disaster zone. There's cut up veggies scattered all over the counter top, peas spilling over the side and onto the floor (many of which have been squashed by Tracy's swollen feet), and I can see the sweat on my wife's brow dripping into the pot of mashed potatoes. There's a cut open squash on the table with brown sugar sprinkled all over the orange insides, and I can't help but notice it's remarkable resemblance to roadkill. Tracy smiles at me and pats my ass, and when she tries to wink at me I feel my pecker shrink to half its size. Poor gal, she truly had forgotten how to be sexy.

"Can you set the table, sweetie?"

"Yea sure," I say, moving towards the cupboards.

"No, no," she stops me, placing a greasy hand on my arm. "Use the good china."

"Why do we have to use the good china, huh?"

"Because Markus, it's a special occasion. Besides, my mother always said you have to dress the part to play the part."

"But, she's blind..."

"That's just like you, no imagination, no sentimentality..."

"Sent – imenta – what?"

"You look at everything so bluntly."

And I let this comment slide, because it would be pointless to try and divulge to her the horrible truth that her mother has never and will never notice the good china, and even if she did, she certainly wouldn't derive any sort of joy from it. You see, my wife still contended that people were overall good creatures, and that karma existed, and that if you were good, good things would happen to you. It really was incredible, her ability to disregard the harsh truths; I'm sleeping with another woman, we probably don't have enough money saved up for retirement, our house is worth 2/3s of what it was when we bought it ten years ago, and, oh yea, she's fucking pregnant again. If karma does exist, then Tracy must have been one evil goddamn kid (and I know for a fact she wasn't).

There's a knock at the door which interrupts my subconscious cynical tirade.

"She's here!" Tracy exclaims. "Markus, can you get it, please?"

I look over at my wife who's currently attempting to mash the boiled potatoes in our giant stainless-steel pot. Her hands are covered up to the elbow in potato paste and when I notice that her lower lip is trembling and there's brown sugar smeared across her one cheek, I guess I feel sort of bad for her and all, so I head towards the front door without a word of protest.

"Hello," Helen's voice echoes from the front entrance. "Isn't anybody going to come help a blind old lady?"

Jesus, here we go.

Tracy shoots me a look and I jump into action, rushing from the kitchen, past all the dyed eggs and fluffy bunnies, past my hipster son still lounging on the couch, and into the foyer.

The front door is swung open and the cab driver is standing awkwardly with Helen hanging off his arm. She is a tiny woman whose back had compressed with each passing year, giving her that hunched over Quasimodo look that so many older women are lucky enough to acquire. Her hair sits upon her head like a dead white bunny rabbit, and the wrinkles in her face remind me of the circles in a tree trunk. Her squinty eyes dart around uselessly in her head and the thought of flicking her in the nose with my index finger crosses my mind, although I'm not exactly proud of it. The cabby gives me a nod as I reach out and take Helen's hand. The cabby's beard is long and black, and I can smell the gallon of cologne he put on this morning wafting from his pours.

"Ma'am," he says with an outstretched hand, "that will be $23.76."

"Twenty-three dollars!" she cries, "I remember when I could get a cab from across town for not more than ten. Are you ripping me off? You know it's terrible karma to rip off a little-old-blind-lady. Especially on Easter!"

"Sorry ma'am, I do not celebrate Easter."

"What are ya, huh, a Muslim?"

"I'm Sikh, ma'am."

"Potato-potautow," says my mother-in-law, maneuvering her wooden stick up between her one armpit and rummaging through her oversized purple purse. "Here you go," she says, producing a five-dollar bill.

The cabby looks at me confused and I can't help but laugh a bit on the inside. Helen holds the five-dollar bill out with the conviction of someone who is used to being in control, and even though I would love to let this little escapade play itself out, I fish out a twenty-dollar bill from my own pocket and hand it over to the cabby.

"Thank you, sir, and er... ma'am," and with that, the cabby turns hurriedly and scuttles back to his car.

"What a nasty beast," Helen says, "I could smell his aftershave the whole ride over."

"It's good to see you, Helen," I say. "Here, why don't we...ow! Goddamnit..."

"Sorry dear," Helen says. I rub my shin and feel the bump from where her stick smacked into it. She was remarkably accurate for a blind woman.

"Hi Mom!" Tracy says, coming into the front and relieving me of my torturous duty. She gives her mother a big hug, and Helen returns it half-heartedly. She did not age with grace, and after her sight began to falter, the bitterness train had been rolling on steadily. She was not a happy older woman (she actually made me seem like an optimist).

"You feel fat," Helen says.

I have to bite my lip to stop myself from laughing.

"Mom! I'm almost seven months pregnant. You know that. "

"Hm," she says. "I never put on that much weight when I was pregnant. And you weren't a tiny baby either, let me tell you that."

"Fuck!" Thomas yells from the living room.

"Thomas!" Tracy yells back, "Turn off the TV and come say hi to your grandmother."

"But mom..."

"Turn off the fucking TV!"

"You people talk like savages, you know that?" Helen muses. "Harold and I never used to speak to each other this way."

Tracy rolls her eyes and I can share in the irony of the statement, because I know that Helen and Harold didn't really talk to each other period. They were the quintessential husband and wife of the 40s. Harold worked construction until his back gave out at fifty-six. He came home half-drunk nearly every night, sat in his favourite arm chair in front of the TV and ate dinner off a TV dinner tray, drank a few more beers, smoked a couple cigarettes and went to bed (and my guess is, the sex was silent and efficient – which begins to sound more appealing to me as I grow older). He used to walk around their house and pick up specs of crumbs from the hardwood floor with the tip of his finger. He was an astute and proper man, which is probably why he never liked me too much. The simple truth is; Helen hasn't had anyone to really talk to in a long time. Harold died over ten years ago, and as her eyes degenerated, so did her overall mood and demeanor (which prevented her from acquiring any new friends).

Thomas enters the front foyer and goes over to Grandma Helen.

"Hi Grandma," he says, hugging her around the shoulders. I'm startled to realize just how much he towers over Helen now.

"You're so big," Helen chimes, "and so skinny!"

"Thanks grandma."

"It's nice to know there's one man in this family who can keep in shape."

And even though I know she has practically zero vision left, she looks directly at me when she says this, smirking blindly at my deflated chest and over-hanging gut. What a bitch. My son pretends to smile (which is pointless considering the old hag is blind), but I can see through his tight lips and contorted face that it pains him.

"Let's go sit down," Tracy says, leading her mother to the dining room table.

"Ow, Fuck's sake!"

"Sorry dear," Helen says as she patters by. "Where is that beastly animal of yours?" I hear her ask Trace as they make their way into the dining room. "He's usually slobbered all over me by now..."

Trace looks back at me and I feel a pang of sadness in my stomach, although I suppose it could just be my liver finally failing.

I stop Thomas as he moves to follow Trace and Helen.

"What the hell was that all about?" I ask him.

"What was what about?"

"You screaming fuck at the top of your lungs in front of your grandmother!"

"Oh," he shrugs, "it's A'ishah."

"Ah, yes," I say, nodding and trying to give a convincing smile, although I'm sure it more resembles the face of a man in the middle of a particularly unpleasant evacuation. "And when is Alicia getting here?"

"Dad, it's A'ishah. And she's going to be late. Apparently, they gave her a hard time at the Greyhound Station, those racist bastards. They demanded she remove her hijab, and wouldn't let her on the bus until she did. It's sickening. I thought Canada was supposed to be progressive!"

"Well, Tommy boy, I guess we ought to start covering our women's faces with towels then, eh? If that's the progressive thing to be doing..."

"You're such an asshole!"

"Debatable."

"Thomas!" Trace pipes in. "Both of you. Enough. It's no problem at all, sweetheart. Alyssa can show up whenever she wants."

"It's A'ishah for Chrissakes!"

I can't help but chuckle, and Thomas shoots me a seething look that could melt ice.

Just then, a knock comes thumping from the front door. Thomas looks at me with fire in his eyes, shrugging his narrow shoulders.

"It can't be her," he says. "She's just getting to the bus station now."

I turn to my wife, who has retreated to the kitchen, peeking her head around the corner of the wall the same way Maximus used to whenever he heard me cracking a beer.

Another knock.

"You didn't..." I start, unable to find the words.

"Markus, he's your father."

My blood is erupting, filling my head with hot bubbles. Stars flash behind my demented eye balls. I feel dizzy. I feel sick. I feel like punching a hole through the goddamn wall. How could she go behind my back like this?

"Markus, he's your father," she says again. "He deserves to be here."

"Tell that to my dead mother!"

"Markus! Don't be so crude. Ping is a part of this family now. She deserves to be here too."

"She's younger than I am!"

"She's a lovely young lady."

"Doesn't it concern you that my father can't even speak a goddamn word of Mandarin, or Cantonese, or whatever the fuck they speak over there in the Philippines – and so far the only English words I've heard her say are 'Hrerro', and 'tank-you prease'."

"Love has no language," my wife says, turning to me as she rises from the table with a triumphant look on her face.

"Is that the title of your new novel?"

"No," she says, "But that's not a bad idea, actually..."

"Jesus..."

I haven't spoken with my father in almost a year. He lives out in Armprior with his new wife. He is married to a woman named Ping. She is from the Philippines and does not know how to put a full sentence together in English (which suits my father just fine). You see, it was about a year and a half ago that Earl started showing up places with Ping, claiming that she was his caretaker.

At first, I actually believed it too.

I thought maybe my father had gone incontinent and was utilizing Ping to help change his goddamn diapers. But no. He soon revealed to me that Ping and he had actually met on an online dating website, and they were in fact very much involved in a sexual relationship. And that wasn't all. He also intended to marry her so as to make her application process for Permanent Residency easier. Oh, and because of love too, I guess. My father took Ping down to Niagara Falls and got the knot tied at a Casino, which was somehow just so utterly fitting I can't really deny the process.

"Dad, you're breathing really loud."

Another knock.

"Mark, answer the door!"

"Fine," I say through gritted teeth, and for a second, I contemplate running up the stairs and hiding in my room with the door slammed tightly shut... Jesus fucking Christ Markus, act like an adult. It feels like I'm walking through quicksand on my way to the front door. I can feel my face getting hot and sweat breaking out on my lower back. I pull the door open and there he is, standing on my goddamn front porch in all his glory, like there was nothing unusual about his being here, smiling his big dumb smile with those twenty-five thousand-dollar dentures sticking out of his lips that are far too square and far too white. He's got one arm around my step-mother, who is about half the size of my father, her lineless face looking much like that of a porcelain doll.

"Hello son!" he booms, moving to embrace me in his usual bear hug.

"Nice to see you, Earl," I say, taking a step back. He looks at me perplexed as I stick out my hand. He takes it reluctantly and frowns, giving it a couple good thrusts.

Earl Stanfield, a standup modern man for the ages. At least he used to be. His once fit frame has digressed to the typical middle-class pre-senior citizen; the round bulge of his pot-belly protrudes out from his tucked in shirt (my father always tucked in his shirts, even t-shirts), the flat ass and skinny legs, hairy forearms and red patches on his cheeks. He has white hair and bushy white eyebrows, and I can only imagine how many pills he has to pop to get his pecker popping for Ping (sorry, but anger tends to bring out the alliterations in me). My mother was diagnosed with Multiple Sclerosis just after her sixty-fifth birthday, and I watched the disease eat away at her motor skills, reducing her to nothing more than a swiveling head atop a shit and piss factory. She died two years ago, and that was the last time I hugged Earl.

"Sorry we're late," my father begins. "Ping wanted to see the Parliament Buildings so we made a quick stop there on our way through. It was her first time seeing them, isn't that right dear?"

"Ah wres, very beautifur!"

"Well, we're very glad you made it," I say, the words barely slipping through my teeth. Ping is twenty years younger than my father, and was more suitable a sister to me than a step-mother.

I lead them into the dining room where Helen is sitting with a gin and tonic, looking particularly miserable and disinterested as my wife explains the premise of her new novel. Thomas is sitting across from Helen with his eyes securely glued to his goddamn cell phone, and for a fleeting moment I think about snatching it out of his hands and smashing it against the fucking wall.

"Hello Trace!" my father says, going in for the hug. Trace obliges, rising from her chair and indulging in ol' Earl Stanfield's famous bear hug. Such a phony bastard.

"So nice to see you, Earl," she says. "It's been too long."

"Indeed," he nods.

"And Thomas," my father booms. He's always had a commanding voice, and the old man knew how to use it. Thomas's neck wrenches upwards and he is suddenly part of the real world again. "You are looking great, son. How much weight have you lost? I bet the girls are all over you at school!"

"Hi grandpa, hi Ping."

"Oh, Herro!"

Earl turns to me then. "It's been far too long, son."

"Yeah, I guess it has."

Ping is standing just behind my father, nodding her head profusely for some unknown reason. I dodge around her and bolt for the kitchen. I walk slowly back into the room with a chair in either hand. My wife has already produced two more plates from our fine china cabinet, and I see my father attempting to introduce Helen to Ping. The two exchange an awkward handshake, Helen's hand floating momentarily in the air like a dangling twig.

"Soa nice to meet chew."

"Earl, where did you meet this... woman?" Helen asks, squinting up at nothing in-particular.

"Helen!" I interject, before my father can begin to explain the intricacies of his online dating relationship. "You look like you need a refresher on that drink of yours."

"As a matter of fact, I do," she says, which makes me think for a second that maybe this old bird isn't half bad. Then again, she was probably acting out of the same necessity as me.

Just then, I hear a slight tapping at the door, barely audible over the sound of the incessant chattering taking place at my dining room table. I watch my son bolt up from his seat and go dashing for the front foyer. I sigh and head into the kitchen, essentially wanting to hide away behind the fridge, bottle in hand, and if Helen wants to join me I'd probably even let her, so long as she didn't speak or whack me in the leg again.

I can hear the muffled sounds of my son greeting his Muslim girlfriend, and I wonder if she's going to remove her head scarf for dinner. I mean, how is she going to eat? I open the bottle of gin and slug back a shot straight from the source, standing over the kitchen sink and staring at the faucet, and for a moment I can see myself spiraling down the drain, washing away with all the dirt and grime from the dishes.

"Hey you!"

I jump nearly a foot in air, twirling around in tremendous fashion to see my pregnant wife smiling up at me, her hands placed firmly on my hips. She leans in for a kiss and I oblige. Her breath tastes of wine and despair (or maybe that was just me).

"Isn't this nice?" she says.

"Yeah, it's... nice. Very nice."

"I'm glad you think so," she says, opening the oven door to check on the turkey.

"Turkey's done," she exclaims. "Do you want to carve it, or should we let Earl do the honour?"

"Let the old man have his day," I say, knowing that such a menial gesture would mean much more to my father than it ever has to me. Fucking rip the legs off the thing with your bare hands and eat it right off the bone for all I cared. Sometimes, I reckon I would have done much better as a Neanderthal or a caveman (although deep down I know that I'm far too pampered to have ever survived the wilderness).

I return to the dining room with my drink and Helen's fresh gin and tonic. I set it down in front of her, and am amazed at the accuracy with which she snatches it up. Must have quite a good nose on her, at least for booze.

I take a seat and proceed to down half of my drink in one malice filled gulp.

"I see your AA meetings are going well," Helen says to me from across the table.

"Well, it's a good thing you don't see too well, Helen."

"Markus!"

"Sorry."

"Oh, it's quite alright, dear. I hear alcoholics tend to be short tempered."

If only it wasn't considered murder to kill your mother-in-law.

My son enters the room with Alissa, and I notice she is not wearing anything over her head or face. She is smiling this dazzling smile, her teeth all white and perfectly lined, and her hazelnut complexion which seems perfectly smooth and nice. She is wearing jeans and a blouse, and for a minute, I wonder if my son was just pulling my leg this whole time, playing a trick on his bigoted old father.

"Everyone, this is A'ishah."

Helen makes some sort of grunt as she is sipping her drink, which I suppose is meant to be a greeting.

Trace rushes from the kitchen and wraps her arms around Asaiah. I notice the startled look on her face at first, all wide eyed and open mouthed, but then she relents and hugs my wife back, which makes me feel sort of good, I guess.

Next up: ol' Earl. He rises from his seat and approaches my son and his girlfriend.

"Hello there Alycia!" he beams, reaching out his hand.

"It's... you know what? Never mind," my son says.

Alycia shakes my father's hand and smiles. Ping has maneuvered herself behind my father, again, and is nodding, again. Her goddamn neck must be getting sore. "This is my wife, Ping."

"Awery nice to meet chew!"

"You as well," Algeria says. Her voice is sultry and deep.

"And this..." my son starts, gesturing towards where I am standing behind my chair, drink in hand, probably looking like a stunned mongoloid. "This is my father."

Alessa approaches me and sticks out her hand for me to take. I do. She has soft hands and a firm handshake, and her smile pierces through me, making me cough and sputter as I try to think of something to say. She was the furthest thing possible from what I had imagined when my son said he had a Muslim girlfriend, and the stark contrast in her appearance with what I had expected... I suppose it causes me to reflect a bit on my perceptions... although I quickly extinguish this dangerous flame of thought before it can really take hold.

"So, um, yea, I thought – my son told me anyways, aren't you, you know? Muslim?"

"Jesus Christ dad."

"I mean... where's your, you know, where's your... scarf?"

For a minute, I feel like I've just taken a giant shit on the table as the air hangs in utter apprehension, the only audible sound is Helen's raspy breathing as she takes another sip from her gin and tonic. But to my relief Alycia laughs, throwing her head back. "I am a Muslim, Mr. Stanfield. I do believe in Allah and I do follow many of the customs and traditions that are asked of us. But I am also a reasonable and grateful person, and I understand what Canada has done for me. For the freedoms I have now been blessed with, and how lucky I am to have escaped my home country, despite how it pains me... thinking about all those left behind. I want to make the best of this."

"So... you don't wear a scarf?"

"It's called a niqab, dad."

"I wear it when I'm with my family and sometimes when I'm out in public. But I am not bound by it. Besides, how would I be able to enjoy this delicious feast we are about to dive into!"

Jesus... is she psychic?

"Your English is very good," my father chimes in, now sitting back in his seat, his hand still on Ping's skinny thigh.

"Thank you, sir. I learned it in Syria, before I came over. I was one of the lucky ones, being able to attend school, although in the end it almost got me killed."

My father grimaces and nods, and an awkward silence hangs in the room for a moment as we all contemplate our mundane first world problems.

93

"Well," Trace says, "why don't you two take a seat, and I'll bring out the turkey!"

My son and Alycia take their seats and after standing dumbly behind my chair for a moment, I finally force my body to start moving and take my seat as well. Helen is squinting across the table at Alissa, and I can only imagine the horrible thoughts flitting through her mind at the moment, and this revelation causes me to question my own opinions, and for a horrid second, I wonder if Helen and I actually have quite a lot in common...

"Earl," my wife says as she carries out the silver turkey tray, "will you do the honours?"

"Thought you'd never ask!"

So, my father gets up and starts carving the turkey, smiling like he's just won the goddamn lottery or something, and I can't help but wonder what chemical imbalance in his brain convinces him that cutting a turkey is so rewarding.

I look around the table; Tracey sitting there smiling a nervous smile as she attempts to interact with her mother; my father, carving the hell outta that turkey and chatting it up with Helen about some irrelevant soap opera; Ping, still nodding and smiling and looking completely clueless; my son, who is whispering in Alena's ear, and I must admit, she is quite beautiful, her dark complexion and jet-black hair. It was like a goddamn United Nations Convention was taking place in my dining room (although in all honesty I'm sure we could probably accomplish more than the UN ever has).

"Oh!" Ping says suddenly, "I loveadees plates!"

"Thank you, Ping," Trace says, glancing in my direction. Goddamn you, Ping.

"Have you ever seen such a big meal over in the Philippines?" I ask.

"Ah, Philippines, wres!"

"Never mind," I say, shaking my head and feeling a cold rage seep into my veins. My face feels hot and I have to consciously make an effort to keep my hands from shaking. I keep my mouth shut for the rest of the meal, which drags on at an excruciatingly slow pace, listening to my father ask Thomas the same questions

Helen already asked, hearing him answer them in the same half-hearted manner, watching Trace attempt to hold a conversation with Ping, who so far has eaten about three bites of mashed potatoes and a couple peas. I watch her pick up the gravy and stare down into the brown liquid with a sort of disgusted fascination. Clearly, she had never seen such a concoction before, and for some reason this irritates me so that I have to pour myself another scotch (at this point I have the bottle situated beside my plate on the dining room table; I am shameless). Helen and my father share a brief conversation about pensions, which inevitably leads to me.

"Yeah, yeah, I should have been a carpenter," I say, brushing them off.

"So, Thomas," my father inquires from across the table. "Have you thought about what you're going to do after school?"

"Yes," Trace chimes in. "Have you thought about your career path?"

"I don't necessarily believe in the modern-day job market," my son announces triumphantly, sitting up all straight in his seat and peering around the room. Here we go, I think to myself, another address from Right Honourable Member.

"We've been conditioned to be consumers our whole lives, and we don't value the proper things anymore. Capitalism has caused us to lose sight of what really matters, because now, all that matters is money. It's all symptomatic of our superficial obsessions, and I'm not really sure I want to be a part of a system that promotes narcissism and materialism."

I watch him glance quickly over at Arianna as he speaks.

"Well, it's a good thing you're majoring in English then," I say, leaning over the table like a hungry hyena. "Because odds are you won't find yourself working in the modern-day job market anytime soon."

"Markus!" Trace hollers at me.

Helen takes a long drink of scotch.

My father stares on concernedly, his eyes shifting frantically from face to face.

Ping sits there smiling.

95

Anita looks at Thomas, and he looks back at her.

And then I start laughing. I cannot control myself. Something about the whole scenario reminds me of a perverted Last Dinner. Da Vinci could have created quite the fucking masterpiece with this lot, that's a goddamn certainty.

Everyone finishes eating and I help my wife carry all the dishes back into the kitchen, not because I am a caring and thoughtful husband; it is simply a way for me to escape the table. From what I can tell, Helen is passed out in her chair, the lucky old hag, her head lolling down towards her chest, breathing heavily through her mouth. I can hear Thomas and his Muslim girlfriend talking about world politics, and the short sightedness of the American Immigration System.

"Oh, I think Clinton is giving a speech right now, we ought to go put it on..."

Fat fucking chance.

"No!" I call back from the kitchen. "I'm sorry, but no speeches. We're watching baseball."

"Basebarr!" I hear Ping exclaim.

"Ping loves baseball," my father says, grinning at me as I re-enter the dining room, moving swiftly through it with a beer in hand, heading for the sanctuary of my reclining La-Z-Boy. I watch Helen come bounding out of her stupor, jolting forward and blinking her squinty little eyes rapidly like a fish that's just been plucked from the water. The turkey and scotch begin their eloquent dance within my stomach, twirling each other around and making me sleepy.

I collapse into my chair and flick on the television. My father and Ping enter and sit down beside each other on the love seat. I can hear Trace telling Helen more about her latest novel, and for Helen's sake, I hope she's passed out again.

Thomas and Alyssa enter the room.

"We're going to go for a walk," Thomas tells me.

"Be my guest," I say. "Enjoy the intricate beauty of our suburban paradise."

To my surprise, Alicia laughs and I watch Thomas glare at me before he leads her from the room.

Tracy and Helen come into the living room, and the two of them take a seat on the couch. Tracy scoops the laptop off the coffee table and opens it with some zest.

"Better check my Facebook Account," she says, beaming. "Here Ma, take a look at this."

I watch Helen squint at the computer screen, moving her face within inches of the computer, and I wonder if this is what Hell is like. Watching blind old souls attempt to read Facebook messages, but alas are never able to decipher the words. For eternity.

"Look here, sweetie," Trace says, turning the laptop in my direction.

Swaying my head around in a listless maneuver, I see a Facebook profile with an ultrasound snapshot as the profile picture. The name above the picture is '? Stanfield.'

"What is this?" I ask.

"It's his or her profile," she says, patting her belly.

"No, you didn't..."

"Oh, don't be such a party-pooper. Look, already got fifteen friends!"

"But, he... or she doesn't even have a name. We don't even know if it's a boy or a girl for Chrissakes!"

"Well I know that, Markus," my wife says, shaking her head at me like I'm the crazy one. "I asked for some suggestions and look, people have been responding – this is so fun!"

I look down the page at the recent posts:

Stanfield:
Hello friends! I can't wait to meet all of you! I am not sure whether I will be a boy or a girl yet, but maybe you can give my mother and father some name suggestions!

Shirley McCafe:
Harold is an excellent name for a young man.

Carolyn Gumble:
I've always loved the name Anastasia.

Ted Rasbin:
OBAMA!!!!!!!

Louise Sheppard:
Sebastian.

I lean back into the couch and try to contain the onslaught of pessimistic rage that is threatening to spew from my mouth. Harold? Anastasia? Who are these fucking people? My wife seems to sense this and turns the computer back around to face her. I watch her face light up as another sound bleeps from the computer, indicating some sort of notification from Fuckbook. Poor '? Stanfield', the baby was doomed before it even got out of the womb.

"Homerrun!" Ping cheers, startling Helen so that she drops her walking stick.

"Mom, you look tired," Trace says.

"Hmm," she groans drunkenly. "I need my own bed."

Trace gathers up her wet puddle of a blind mother and makes for the door. Before she leaves she signs out of her Facebook and closes the computer, looking at me as if she were locking a goddamn safe and expected me to avert my eyes. If only she truly knew how uninterested I was with any aspect of her life, especially her online existence.

Trace says her goodbyes and I hear the door shut. Ping sits there complacently with this stiff sort of smile held up on her lineless face, while my father clears his throat repeatedly, and I can only assume he is attempting to think of something significant to say, something memorable, something epic. He was a corny mother fucker.

"Your mother would be so happy we're all here together," he says finally, turning to me.

"Don't talk about mom."

"I can remember how she used to make us all go for a walk after dinner," he says, ignoring my previous comment. "God, we used to bitch and moan about those walks, but looking back at them

98

now, I suppose they were some of the happiest times of my life. Remember I used to give you piggy-backs? And sometimes we would jump in the giant piles of leaves, or snow if it happened to be Christmas. No matter what, we had to go for a walk after a big family dinner. She was a real fire-cracker. You couldn't tell her no when she set her mind to something. But you know what? I hardly ever wanted to say no to her anyways. She was good like that. She knew how to take care of people..."

He turns to me then, waiting for me to say something.

"You are so full of shit," I say.

"Mark, you know I miss your mother more than anything..."

"Yea, clearly..."

"Markus..."

"You replaced mom with a fucking China Doll!"

My father looks down at his chest, then over towards Ping, then back at me.

"I guess we should be going," he says.

"Yeah, but it was soooo nice having you two here. Really brings back good memories, ain't that right Ping?"

"Oh-oh, ah, tank-you, prease."

"You might want to teach her that people in North America usually say either thank you, or please, not both put together, eh pops?"

He grimaces and frowns, opens his mouth to say something, then thinks better of it.

Monday

Hiding within the confines of my office has become a secret pleasure, as sad as that may sound. Away from all the sounds and sights of my household; my anti-establishment son who sits fighting the power in his mind while he conforms with the masses by staring at his goddamn cell phone all day long; my pregnant wife who is planning for her baby shower tomorrow, which I have somehow been suckered into taking part in. It's a sad state of affairs when a man feels more at home in his office than in his home, but here we are folks, may as well make the best of it!

My phone jumps into life on the desk.

I scoop it up with frantic gestures and open the text message from Cheryl. The message says: hope this can take your mind off work for a minute or two. There is a picture attached and I open it with adulterous intentions (I can feel blood rushing to my cock and make a mental note that I am indeed wearing dress pants right now and I have Mr. and Mrs. Scholace scheduled to meet me here any minute). She is standing in front of a mirror, fully clothed in a dark purple blouse and a white skirt that wraps tightly around her slender hips. Her face is scrunched up a bit and she has her skirt hiked up about an inch short of where her special spot starts.

I hear the bell ring from the front door, and I start to stand up, but realizing the precarious position my pants are currently poking out at, I decide it's best to wait at my desk.

The two of them come strolling right in, past my non-existent secretary, and stand together in my office doorway, staring at me with the blank faces of brain hungry zombies. God, I hated married couples. I wait for them to say something, but it would appear they are waiting for me to make the first move, and I try to relish in this inadvertent game of chicken that we are playing.

My phone buzzes again in my hand and I look down quickly to see another message from Cheryl. She is now down to her bra and panties, sitting up on her desk with her legs splayed out, playing with herself.

"Mr. Stanfield," they say in unison. "May we get started?"

"Oh, you betcha. In fact, I'm already pretty well started over here."

They look at me quizzically, and I wonder to myself if I've ended up with the two most boring people on the planet as clients. The charming couple is sporting attire which would be more suitable upon the shoulder of my dead grandparents. Josh is wearing a wool brindle vest and the lovely Mrs. Scholace is looking absolutely bulbous in a multi-coloured cardigan with white puffy pants.

God, they were utterly boring... but it was the boring ones who were dangerous. They were slow, meticulous, and risk adverse (pretty much a real estate agent's worse nightmare, or any salesman for that matter).

"Well, shall we get going?" Mr. Scholace asks, looking at his gold watch. "We have doctor appointments at 4pm, so it'd be best we make haste."

"And make haste we shall," I say, wondering if perhaps these two had come through some sort of portal ripped open the space-time continuum. "As soon as I... huh, why don't you two meet me out front, I'll just be a minute, I have to... um, sharpen my pencil."

Again, they stare at me as if I'm some sort of impressionist painting that they can't quite figure out, meanwhile, I'm slowly rubbing my cock beneath my desk, urging the little pecker to relent and return to its docile state of staring at the floor. The two leave and I am left to my own devices. I hear the bell on the front door again, and shrug my shoulders as I decide to get on with it. Certainly, this isn't the first time I've 'sharpened my pencil' in the office, and I can bloody well guarantee you it won't be the last (unless of course I happen to swerve into oncoming traffic on the way to the showing, taking Mr. and Mrs. Scholace with me to the fiery pits of hell, in which case I'm sure I'd be free to sharpen my goddamn pencil for eternity, and that suits me just fine, if you must know).

That night, I'm lying in my bed alone, butt-naked, trying to figure out how to take a dick-pic (as the kids call them these days). Trace is out shopping for the baby shower tomorrow with Thomas and I have the house to myself. Why a nineteen-year-old boy would want to accompany his mother as she shops for baby shower accessories is beyond me, but I'm learning to disregard the things about my son of which I have no understanding (because let's be honest, I don't understand a fucking thing about him).

My one hand is coated in Vaseline (as well as my cock, balls and most of my lower torso) and I've got my cell phone out with the other hand, trying to angle it correctly so that my dick looks as big as physically possible in the picture. Cheryl has sent me numerous pictures of her tits, her cunt, even one of her asshole (me thinks the young lady enjoys taking these pictures, and she should. She had a glorious vagina), and she was expecting a little reciprocation. I've almost got the perfect shot when, oops, the phone slips from my hand and lands on the floor. Without thinking, I lunge after it, wiping Vaseline and my own spit all over the bed spread, and like an idiot I scoop up the phone with my filthy hand covered in gelatin and bodily fluids. The screen is smeared with a thick glob of Vaseline and I can't help but laugh. New toys clearly were not made for old timers, and as far as I can tell, this dick-pic operation has failed miserably. I go to the bathroom to wash myself up (which takes considerable effort, as any guy who's used Vaseline to jerk-off can tell you). After using about half a roll of toilet-paper, I've managed to remove most of the sticky shit from my dick, balls, torso and cell phone. I take a look in the mirror, standing here stark naked, and I can't help but be horrified at what I see. What once used to be a formidable chest with tight skin and the hints of definition has now mutated into a flabby and disgusting mess. My pecks (or more accurately, tits), aren't quite sagging, but the threshold looks dangerously close to breaking, probably only one more cheeseburger away from the dreaded man-titties. My gut hangs over at my waist in a leering pose, ridiculing me with the fact that I can't see my own cock without sucking it in a bit. I never had a six-pack, but I never used to have this goddamn flat tire either. I try to think of the last time I was at the gym, and am disturbed to realize it's been at least two years (you'll go next week, was the common excuse I gave myself now-a-days). Where did my ambition go?

I return to the bedroom and snatch my pair of abandoned boxer-shorts from the floor.

Flipping through the pictures now stored on my phone, I finally find one that seems suitable enough to send off to Cheryl. It's a bit blurry, but blurry is good for an out of shape and average cock-sized guy like me. Jesus, was there such thing as privacy anymore? It takes me about five minutes to hit the send button. She's seen your nasty ass naked plenty of times by now and she's still fucking you, so what damage can this little picture really do? Fair enough. I hit send and lie back down on the bed. Suddenly, a horrible image flashes through my mind; Thomas, spread out on his bed enacting the very same sloppy procedure I had just attempted. Had the little fucker ever sent a dick-pic out? Jesus, being a parent was a fucking nightmare. At least he's not a girl, says the sinister voice buried at the back of my brain. But this next one could be.

"No," I say out loud. "Please lord, no."

How many fathers were there in the world with a daughter who had naked pictures of herself somewhere on the internet? The thought makes me queasy. What if some impotent pricked old bastard was cruising through Pornhub one night, his cock popping from the hit of Viagra he took just in order to masturbate, and he comes across a particular video that looks appealing, something along the lines of 'virgin gets anal cherry popped,' or 'interracial gangbang schoolgirl,' and he opens it up, ready to dive right in, but just as his weathered hand grasps his tool, he realizes that the little slut he's watching take it up the ass on the internet is actually his own daughter. I wonder if that's ever happened? Probably. And the sad truth is; I'm sure the old perverted bastard wouldn't even notice. Men were animals of impulse, you see, and when our instincts are tuned into beating off, you better stay the fuck out of our way.

I debate whether or not to finish myself off with a little porno session on the computer, or perhaps I could wait for Trace to get home... and I find myself reaching for the computer before this latter thought can complete itself.

I get a text message from Dick around 8:30pm. I'm sitting on the living room couch in my boxers watching an A&E special on OJ Simpson.

Barbarella's. Come now. Drinks on me.

While the context is quite standard for Dick, the demanding nature of the text suggests he is in a bad state. My suspicions are confirmed when I receive a second text a few minutes later. The message consists of one word; fuck.

I call Trace and she reveals that her and Thomas are having dinner at some new Vegan restaurant in the Glebe.

"Oh Markus, you would just love it! It's very chique. So modern and fun, I'm loving it."

"But... there's no meat. Not even cheese?"

"It's vegan, Markus. It's unique."

"Yeah, well, Caitlyn Jenner is unique too, doesn't mean I want to try that."

"You're a party pooper," my wife says, sighing into the phone. There was a time in our lives, way back before Thomas came bursting from my wife's vagina, when she would have laughed at that joke. But she didn't laugh at my jokes anymore, which only strengthens my resolve to hit the strip club with the Dick. I make some elaborate story detailing a last-minute mortgage offer that has gone south, imminent paperwork is required, and I will have to run to the office for a couple of hours.

"Okay sweetheart, we'll see you when you get home."

Was it supposed to be that easy? Did she even care anymore? It was a distressing question that failed to resonate any sort of emotional response within me. I put on a dress shirt that still fits (my closet is littered with old clothes that can no longer contain

104

my girth), toss on my nicest pair of jeans (that still fit), some black loafers, and I am officially strip club ready.

We meet at the Lion's Cock for a quick nip before heading over to the ballet. The place is for the most part deserted on a Monday night, save for a few gangly university students sitting in the middle of the room wearing checkered shirts and tight pants. I overhear them talking about the tyrannical former Prime Minister, comparing him to Hitler and using the usual hyperboles which the liberal education system seems so intent on promoting. My son would fit right in with them.

I find Dick tucked away in our usual corner at the bar.

"You look like you haven't slept in a couple days," I say as I pull up a seat beside him.

"No, no, I passed out at some point last night," he says, as if this is somehow a good thing. "It's not the lack of sleep. It's... just... can we please get the fuck out of here though? Seriously, I feel like I'm going to go on a rampage."

"Okay, okay, just tuck your goddamn pants into your socks and give me a minute."

I'm still not sure what's got Richard the Dick in such a foul mood, but it seems irrelevant at the moment. All I know for sure is that I need a beer. The same surly bartender with the presumably formidable bush takes my order and gives me this strange sort of scowl when I ask for the bill to come with my pint. Yup, definitely taken one too many sour dicks.

"What's got you so pissed off anyways?"

"The Chinese pulled out of the deal," he sighs.

"I hate when they pull out," I say, grinning. Although Dick doesn't seem to notice my cunning innuendo.

"Yes, evidently, they had no intention of hiring Canadians for the project. They accidentally included a couple confidential sheets in their proposal package which highlighted their plans to import workers from China through our Temporary Foreign Worker Program."

"Go figure."

"They are suing us now."

105

"Pardon?"

"The Chinese Government is suing us."

"Who is the 'us' in that sentence?"

"Us. The Canadian Government."

"So... Canadian taxpayers?"

"Essentially."

"How the hell is that even possible?"

"Well, we signed a Foreign Investment Promotion and Protection Agreement with them a couple years back, and one of the clauses buried within the four-hundred-page document allows one state to sue the other if it is perceived that government interference resulted in the loss of revenue."

"Sounds like a pretty shitty deal."

"In hindsight everything can be made to seem shitty..."

"That's some astute political analysis there, Dick."

"Can you fuck off for once?" he says, turning to me with a twisted-up face. It's at this point that I realize he is not joking, and so I decide it's best to keep my mouth shut.

I slug back my beer while Richard sits all hunched over and sulking, staring down at his empty beer glass as if it might contain the meaning of life. Maybe it did. Emptiness. Despair. Desperation.

Sounds about right.

I signal to the bartender and pay for our drinks. She gives me a half-assed smile and returns to looking at her cell phone.

"Let's roll," I say, startling the Dick out of his half-coma. He gives his head a shake and slowly rises to follow me out the door. Dick lights up a dart and I watch him inhale the damn thing in about three puffs. I haven't had a cigarette in almost a year, but I could certainly use one right now.

"Give me one of those," I say, smacking him on the arm.

He hands over a cigarette and his lighter. The smoke fills my lungs and I can feel that familiar tingle, the rush to the head, erasing the pain and sorrow for at least a moment. I suppose that's all we can do in this life. Cope with the pain and sorrow for the briefest of moments, just long enough to keep your sanity before returning to the realities of your disheveled life. After my second drag I start coughing and throw the cigarette on the ground, stomping it out with my heel.

Dick is leaning against the wall with his hands in his pockets looking down at his shoes. The wind picks up for a moment, causing his untucked dress shirt to billow.

"Well, you sure you want to hit the strip club on a Monday, Dick?" I ask him.

"Barbs," he says, waving his hand and walking past me. "We're going to Barbs."

We head west on Sparks down to Kent and hang a left. It's not a far walk. Barbarella's Cabaret was a particularly greasy strip bar which just so happened to be placed conveniently close to Parliament Hill (I mean... you know what I mean). It was the kind of place where you wouldn't want to leave your drink at your table when you went to the washroom, for fear of someone spitting in it (or worse). But it was dark and the beer was cheap and the girls were certainly sexy when they were on stage, so long as you weren't close enough to see their teeth or skin.

We don't really say much to each other on the way, passing by the odd business man in a suit doing his best to look urgent. So many mannequins. Carbon-copied, sealed and faxed (well, I guess no one really uses faxes anymore). Why do we strive to be so similar? Whatever happened to individuality? I suppose it doesn't matter, so long as you get the new iPhone (and you better be damn sure to update your Facebook page announcing it to the world, you could even take a picture of your phone and then post the picture of your phone with your phone, wouldn't that be neat?).

We pass by a homeless gentleman on the corner of Lyon and Sparks who has empty space were teeth should be and is in desperate need of a bath. He holds his little ripped up coffee cup out to Dick, and I watch Dick smack the cup out of the homeless man's hands, his change scattering all along the sidewalk and down onto the road.

"Hay-yer-fuckin-asshhole!" the man yells.

"Get a fucking job," Richard says, spitting back behind his shoulder.

And I can't help but notice the frame by frame frown that sneaks upon the man's face, only there for a moment, and it looks like he might be the saddest man on the planet. He bends over in a stiff and uncomfortable looking way, struggling to pick up his coins while muttering nonsense to himself. The wind picks up and I watch his little coffee cup go spiraling down the road. He reaches for it at first, but realizing his utter and definite defeat, the man simply stops, shuffles backwards, and collapses onto the sidewalk, leaning his back up against a mailbox and resting his chin on his chest.

I stoop down and hand the man a twenty-dollar bill. 'There you go, man,' I say. He nods at me and then looks up to the sky, perhaps searching for some sort of sign... but there's only that grey-blue blanket of dusk to answer him.

Richard is now a full block ahead of me, not bothering to slow down and wait. I've never seen him like this before, and it strikes me that it's finally happening. His mid-life crisis has finally arrived, and the Dick was having a hard time dealing with it. In my opinion, a mid-life crisis is that essential moment when you realize that everything you do, everything you've done, well it doesn't really count for shit. There is a finite time we have here on earth, and you've spent the last twenty or thirty years wasting it.

I watch the Dick go storming in through the black-tinted door of the strip-club and I hustle my lethargic ass to catch up. The light is dim and the bouncer doesn't bother IDing me since I look like a caricature of every middle-aged man that has ever lived. Dick posts up at the bar. The place is mostly empty save for a few older gentlemen sitting closer to the stage in the middle of the room, and a couple of black fellas sitting in the back corner. One of them notices me looking at him and catches my gaze. I turn away instantly.

I pull up a seat beside Dick and neither of us says anything until the waitress comes over. We both order double rye and cokes, and when she asks us how our day is going, we both shrug and say 'okay.'

"Do you think this one here has ever had a kid?" Dick says,

leaning over towards me. He gestures with his head up onto the stage.

"Absolutely not," I say. "Have you ever seen a vagina that's been through that kind of trauma? It takes its toll, let me tell you. Imagine the inside of a rotten mango, a lot more mushy and asymmetrical."

"That's fucking disgusting," Dick says.

"You're welcome," I say bowing my head.

"Jesus, I'm glad I'm not your fucking kid."

"Yeah, well – what would you know about it?"

"Mark, you don't even know your own son," he starts, his hands gesturing in the air like he was addressing some packed room of dignitaries in Parliament. "You sit around bitching about him all the time, and you don't even know the guy. I mean, you thought he was gay for Chrissakes, and now you're telling me he's got some little Arab girlfriend... you've got to take more interest in your family, man."

"Dick, have you ever had children?"

"No, you know that."

"Exactly, so don't presume to give me advice on my son."

Fucking politicians. Always trying to consult people on things which they know nothing about.

The two of us stay silent for a while, drinking begrudgingly from our glasses that likely have pussy residue coating the rims. I sigh and look around the room again. I notice the neon lights hanging above the stairwell that say 'Private Rooms' and I wonder if anyone's ever gone up there just to cry, you know, just for a little privacy?

"I slept with a nineteen-year-old the other night," Richard says to me suddenly, the bass from the speakers thumping inside my chest.

"Congratulations."

"Fuck you, Mark."

"Wow, calm down, Dick. You know I'm serious when I tell you that I envy your life. What have you got yourself all messed up about, anyways?"

"My mother has cancer."

"Shit."

"Yeah."

That awkward, post-cancer announcement silence hangs between us as we finish our third drinks.

"She's had it for almost six months, can you believe that? She's had it for six months and she just told me last weekend."

"It's a tough thing to deal with, Dick..."

"She said she didn't want to bother me with it. She said I was living my life and she didn't want to interrupt anything."

"Well, that's what mother's do, man. They put us first. They always have and they always will. It's their curse."

"But she wouldn't have been interrupting anything!" he says, and I can see his eyes watering up a bit. "I've got fucking nothing going on. Nothing. No family, no kids, not even a fucking cat or dog. I got a goldfish a few years ago and the fucking thing died the second week in. She wouldn't have been interrupting anything."

"You've got a career, a great condo downtown Ottawa, a university degree, you're doing good, man, you're..."

"No, none of that shit matters. Not compared to this. And what if she dies? What if she dies and I never gave her a grandkid, or a wedding? Why should she be proud of me? I haven't done anything. My job is a joke, you know it, and I know it. Hell, anyone who works for the government knows. We stick it out until our pensions kick in, and then we leave our offices in such shit storms that it takes whoever comes in after us at least two years to catch up! The system is fucked. It's the same shit over and over and over..."

"That's not your fault though, Dick."

"Give me another drink," he barks at the bartender. The big-breasted girl with the tight black shirt scowls at us and moves across the bar, thrusting Dick's fresh drink towards him and spilling a bit of it onto his white sleeve.

"You bitch."

"You better watch it, buddy."

"Or what, you'll devour me with your gaping twat?"

At that moment, Rich the Dick is pulled clear off his stool by the massive bouncer with the goatee who has been lingering around listening to our entire conversation. Richard stumbles and flails his arms around as the bouncer drags him roughly from the back of his neck, clamping down so hard I can see Richard's eyes bulging out of their sockets, his face turning red.

"Get the fuck off me you gorilla," he yells. "Umph!"

The punch to Richard's gut leaves him reeling and silent, now clutching at his belly as the big bouncer in the black t-shirt continues to drag him towards the door. I nod awkwardly at the bartender who is staring daggers at me.

"He's having a tough day," I say, shrugging.

"Can you just get the fuck out of here, please?"

"Yes, ma'am."

I slug back my drink and follow the bouncer towards the door. I notice the half-naked girl on stage has stopped her little dance routine and is staring blankly over at us. I give her a wave and keep moving. I watch the bouncer swing the door open with his shoulder and toss Richard out into the fading light. I hear him land hard against the pavement, and he groans as the bouncer begins to turn around. He gives me a menacing look as I shuffle past him.

I go over to help Richard up but he shakes me off. Pulling himself into a sitting position, he begins prodding at his bruised and swollen face. There is a small trickle of blood coming from out of his one nostril, and he looks up at me then, a gray and emotionless face half shadowed in the dim light, and he says, "I wish I had a family to go home to."

Tuesday

Natalie is the first one to show up, naturally, and she has brought a gigantic basket filled up with diapers, baby food, baby bottles, baby clothes, and even some little baby moccasins. She comes bursting in through the door without knocking and as she walks past me on the couch, dumps the damn basket full of baby shit on my lap.

"Big news, Marky boy!" she says, beaming.

"Oh yeah?" I say, feigning interest while taking an unnecessarily large gulp from my rye and coke.

"I am now a single woman!"

"You don't say?"

"The spark was gone. Simple as that. Bob just wasn't doing it for me anymore. And life is too short to spend pretending to love someone, wouldn't you agree?"

"You do you, girl," I say. At least she was finally calling him Bob.

My wife, overhearing Natalie, comes stalking down the stairs with her hair all done up, and it makes me sad to see the look of anxiety on her face. Her nervous smile, and the way her lipstick sits all splotchy upon her swollen lips. The baby bump is ever present, erupting through her black dress like a giant tumor.

"There's the girl of the hour!" Natalie proclaims.

Tracy blushes and bats a hand at her friend, who then proceeds to talk about herself for the next twenty minutes, while I am forced to sit complacently in my spot and fiddle with my fingers, trying my best to keep my damn mouth shut as Natalie prattles on and on about how liberated she feels. Why couldn't they have waited one extra day? At least then I could have gotten drunk with Bob while the hens clucked.

"Mom's here!" Tracy exclaims.

Oh joy. In what world is it fair that I am subjected to seeing my Mother-in-law twice in three days?

"Markus, can you?"

"Yes Mark, be a good husband why don't you," Natalie chimes in. She really was the bane of my existence.

I rise with some effort and make my way to the door, realizing that I am more than slightly inebriated as I stumble over my own two feet, nearly face planting in the foyer. Trace shoots me a look that could shrivel Ron Jeremy's cock.

Composing myself, I fling back the door with the most stretched out and forced smile plastered upon my face that I can muster.

"It's good to see you, Helen," I say. "Here, why don't we...ow! Goddamnit..."

"Sorry dear."

"Hi Mom!" Tracy says, coming into the front and wrapping her increasingly flabby arms around her frail mother.

"You still feel fat," Helen says.

"Helen, can I get you a drink?" I interject.

"That would be fine, Mark."

"Fantastic."

I escape the living room to mix Helen a stiff gin and tonic, three-fingers worth ought to do the trick (she was tolerable enough when she was loaded). I catch my reflection in the window above the sink, all faint and whispering, and I can't help but wonder if this phantom of my figure is actually what remains of my soul.

"Dad," my son calls from the living room. I reenter holding Helen's gin and tonic, and Thomas looks up from his phone with urgent eyes. And by the tone of his voice, the sweet infliction he is purporting to convey, I can tell he is about to ask me for something. "Do you think I could borrow the car for a couple days and go see A'ishah in Kingston?"

"And how exactly would I be able to get to work without my car?"

"You could use mom's I thought..."

"We sold your mother's car last year, don't you remember?"

Thomas looks at me with blank eyes and shrugs. I'm not surprised he doesn't remember, considering we didn't tell him. I needed the extra money to cover his goddamn tuition. Trace started crying when I told her. Are we in trouble? She asked me. No, no, I said. No trouble at all. Meanwhile, I've been ignoring calls from Visa for the past five months, and have developed a routine of hiding unpaid bill notices beneath the spare tire in the trunk of my car (that reminds me, probably time for a backyard bonfire...). Our mortgage is three months behind, and I am waiting for the day that Ottawa Hydro shuts off our power, because I haven't paid that in about four months.

But yeah, things are going great!

At least we'll be able to get some free fucking diapers out of this little party. Hurray!

The guests start rolling in; Hilary and Mariana (both former colleagues who used to work with Tracey), there's Kristina, our neighbor from a couple doors down whom I have literally never said more than two words to since we moved here fifteen years ago (hey, don't blame me, blame the internet), Janice, my wife's second cousin who only shows up for these sorts of frivolous events (family reunions, thanksgiving dinners, you know, all that shit) but is never actually around when Trace needs her, a couple of Natalie's friends show up bearing giant bags of diapers. All of them are also former colleagues of Trace's, and part of me is convinced they are only here to get a look at the crazy one who had a meltdown at work. The two of them are dressed up as if they are heading downtown to the Byward Market for an evening with the university students (do middle-aged women realize how scary they look with all that make-up plastered on their faces?), and finally, that appears to be all of them because the hens start opening up presents at this point, continuing to cluck away at one another, peck-peck-peck, and I can feel my peck-peck-pecker shrinking with the onslaught of overly dramatized stories and outlandish comparisons being made by the gaggle of women

114

currently saturating my living room. They talk about who's gotten fat, who's gotten skinny... they reminisce about their first pregnancies (a lot of disgusting fart stories mixed with grotesque imagery that was far scarier than any horror movie you'd ever seen). Then, inevitably, they start talking about marriage. Fucking marriage.

"My little Rachel is getting married next month," Hilary says, beaming. "Do you believe it?"

At this point I have to literally bite my tongue. Yes Hilary, I can believe it, considering it's the only goddamn thing you've talked about for the past year.

"Oh, that's so exciting!" Mariana exclaims.

"I've been watching your countdown on Facebook!" my wife chimes in.

Oh Tracey... and to think, I actually used to be quite fond of you.

"Marriage is the death of desire," Natalie interjects, arms crossed, sitting there alone on the love couch which I can only assume is a true sign from God. "Look at Bob and I..."

"You mean Robert?"

"...we hadn't had sex in over five months."

"That's just unfortunate," Kristina pipes in. "But I do know what you mean. Seems to be the common story these days."

I try to think back to the last time my wife and I had sex (made love, fucked, fornicated, executed coitus, humped, smashed, banged), and it pains me to realize that before she got pregnant, we probably hadn't fucked in over a year (why couldn't I have just waited for her goddamn uterus to fall out?).

"I feel so liberated!" Natalie screams, her arms in the air and everything, like she was Moses parting the goddamn sea.

And Trace looks at me with a sly grin, rolling her eyes as if to say, she just doesn't know what we have baby. No one knows, they never will. Our love is perfect.

You poor, poor woman.

"And how are you handling all of this, Markus?" Janice asks me suddenly.

"Oh well," I say, struggling with the spotlight now securely fixated on me, their eyes like giant searchlights. "It's going swell. Really good."

"Oh, such a good husband," Mariana croons.

The women all gush in agreement, nodding their heads like chickens pecking for grain.

"And how is work going? You know my husband and I were just talking the other night about the idea of potentially selling our house..."

The idea of potentially selling... Oh yes, please, entice me more with your indecisiveness. Undoubtedly you and your husband have the potential to maybe, quite possibly, be just about the best clients ever!

Don't be stupid Mark, you need every goddamn client you can snatch up. Have you forgotten that nice little letter from the bank with the word FORCLOSURE printed in bold red letters and circled with red pen by a faceless person in a suit? They are coming for you, Marky boy, to take your house – unless of course you can somehow figure out how to get some poor sap to buy a house in this sellers' market.

"You know my number," I say, fingering my collar and taking another sip from my drink.

All I ever wanted was to retire and do nothing at all. Was that too much to ask?

"Oh my," my wife exclaims, feeling at her swollen belly. "I think..."

"Trace, don't move," I tell her.

The room is suddenly silent, all the air being sucked from it like a popped balloon. The look upon the faces of the half-drunk women says it all; wide-eyed with mouths gaping.

"Mark, I think my water just broke..."

Natalie looks at me with watering eyes, while Tracey's mom stares blankly at her daughter with a frown. I try to speak but the words are caught in my throat. The blood trickling down my wife's inner thigh drips upon the hardwood floor, creating a glimmering red pool.

"Mark, what's the matter?"

And then she looks down, screaming into her hands before she begins frantically clutching at her belly, rubbing at it and breathing in this really hysterical and horrifying sort of way, her fingers sticky with blood, and I can feel the blood draining from my own face, the flesh all hot and tingling. My son looks up at me with wide eyes, his lip trembling, and for an instant I see myself in the past, twenty years ago, standing in our old home, looking down at Trace as her water broke, and that feeling of elation and anxiety is so palpable I can almost taste it, like sour wine, an itch at the back of your throat, all your hopes and dreams personified in this very moment, and a black wave washes over me as I realize how much I was truly looking forward to having another child, and just how miserable my life had become without one in it.

Natalie is parading around the room with her arms flailing in the air, yelling at no one in particular, one of the ladies is shrieking, while Tracey's mother sits there squinting and sipping at her drink, looking completely uninterested. This is what hell looks like. Thomas gets to his feet, goes to take a step forward, and then freezes. He turns his head and locks eyes with mine, perhaps hoping that I can offer some sort of unspoken moral support, but apparently my eyes look as bugged out as his, because he turns away quickly with a contorted face, while my wife writhes on the couch, her legs in the air, hands on her belly, and blood pouring from between her legs.

Walking in through the sliding doors, I remember staring at the giant white H above the entranceway and thinking 'welcome to Hell.'

I make my way to the elevator. There's a slack-jawed man in a wheelchair being rolled out as I enter, and I step aside to give them room to pass. The woman pushing him gives me a grievous nod, and I can't help but notice the drool spilling from the corner of the man's mouth, his eyes looking everywhere at once.

I get in the elevator and I hit the fourth-floor button for the ICU. I remember wishing for the elevator to get stuck as it made its slow ascent. There'd be a sweet sort of irony if I were to die in a hospital elevator, like getting hit by an ambulance.

The nurse at the front desk of the ICU greets me by name, and I nod to her as I move past. My eyes feel swollen and I'm afraid that my voice will get caught in my throat if I try to speak. Like a hose spraying dust. I did appreciate the fact that the lights were always a bit dimmer in the ICU, unlike the first floor of the hospital. I guess when it came down to it, no one wanted to shine too much light on death.

My mother was in room 412. She had a room all to herself, which I think was a courtesy afforded to patients who were dying.

I always paused before entering, trying to prepare myself. It never worked though. Her head would always twitch in this frantic sort of way whenever I came in, and it made me want to turn around and run. The MS had obliterated her motor skills at this point, and soon, she would forget how to breathe.

My father was sitting there beside her bed, both of his hands clasped around the bundle of meat and bone which used to be my mother's hand. His eyes were always red, and I hated the way he looked up at me almost more than my mother, like a wounded puppy dog who just got caught pissing on the carpet.

"How's she doing today?"

"The same."

I nodded. Why did death come with so many solemn nods? It seemed a mockery to me. I'll be shaking my fucking head when I die, I can promise you that.

My father got up then because he started to cry. Ma had made it explicitly clear that we were not to cry in front of her at the hospital, and so more often than not, my father spent most of his time leaning against the wall in the hallway with his head buried in his hands, softly sobbing as nurses and doctors pattered past, pretending not to notice him. Sometimes, I pretended not to notice him too.

And at the funeral, when he tried to hug me in front of the casket, I guess that's why I pushed him away. I blamed him. For everything. And I guess I still do.

I went over to his seat and resumed his position beside Ma. I tried reading to her some nights, back when her motor functions had first betrayed her. But I couldn't do it. I'd be sitting there beside her hospital bed, the dim hospital light hanging above, surrounded by foreign beeps and alien noises of the machines which were keeping my mother alive, reading her a Tom Clancy novel, and I would look up from the page and catch her looking at me with frantic eyes. I could always tell she wanted to say something, because her hand would twitch or her leg would move sporadically, and after looking again into her contorted face, the tears would start falling uncontrollably, which would force me to leave the room.

So yeah, I didn't bring books with me to the hospital anymore. I don't think she could hear or understand too well at that point anyways.

I remember I sat there, staring out the window at the grey-blue sky, and I could hear my mother trying to swallow, and having quite a time of it, gurgling and choking on her own spit, and it made me want to smash a hole in the goddamn wall.

"Ma," I started, trailing off. The doctor had made it pretty clear, without being too insensitive, that my mom was on her last legs. 'Any day now,' I believe was the phrase he used.

I was trying to think of something meaningful to say. Something poignant and elegant that would sum up all of the beautiful and wretched feelings swimming amidst the whiskey and beer within my gut. My eyes were burning and I could feel my goddamn lip trembling, so I actually stood up and walked over to the corner of the room where she couldn't see me, and I slapped myself in the face, hard, repeatedly, until my lip stopped flittering.

I returned to her bedside and stood over her, looking into her bloodshot eyes and softly brushing her forearm.

"You've always been the most important person in my life," I started. "You're pretty much the only person who's always had my back, and I don't think... it's just, that sort of thing, it doesn't come along all too often, you know?"

"This is such fucking bullshit..." I said, choking a bit. "I guess I'm just angry. I've been meaning to make it up to you, you know? I was supposed to do more, with my life, with my aspirations and my dreams. My writing. But I gave up. I stopped trying. But deep down, I always thought I'd get another chance, you know? To make it up to you. To make you proud..."

I started crying then, so I had to leave. I walked past my father who was all crouched up against the wall outside the door, and went to the bathroom. It stunk like chemicals, as hospital bathrooms always do. I wiped my eyes and starred at myself in the mirror for a while, like a boxer about to hit the ring. And then I went back and sat beside ma some more, said goodbye, and left.

She died that night.

And those were the last things I ever said to her... and I don't even know if she fucking heard me. If she could understand...

Sometimes, I have nightmares about being trapped in the ICU. Trapped up on the fourth floor of the hospital, running down never-ending hallways as my mother's disembodied voice calls out my name, and in the end, I can never find her fucking room.

People like to say that time heals all wounds, but from what I can tell, the more time that goes by, the angrier I get, because I keep picturing these little scenarios, these tiny moments in my every day life, and I find myself thinking 'if only ma was here to see this...' and I guess, if anything, the more time that drifts on has only made me more bitter, and every time I think that maybe I'm getting over it, something else will happen that reminds of just how much shittier the world is without her in it.

My mind feels detached from my spine; drifting.

Sitting here in the all-white waiting room of the hospital emergency lobby, the teal coloured cushions of the uncomfortable chairs seem somehow repulsive to me. The walls are a dull beige (beige keeps people calm, Trace told me once). Why did hospitals have to seem so robotic? The stainless steel, the constant beeping and buzzing of the machines, it always made me feel cold.

Every sound I hear makes me jump, and fifteen minutes ago a woman started screaming from somewhere down the hall, a horrid and high-pitched shriek, and all I can think of is how sorry I feel for myself.

I feel translucent as the florescent lights above shine down upon me. Thomas is sitting beside me, staring down at his goddamn phone. His apparent disinterest infuriates me and so I snap at him to turn off his fucking phone. He looks up at me with tears in his eyes and I realize he's crying, and that I am probably the worst fucking father on the planet.

"It's okay," I say, reaching out my hand and placing it on his shoulder. Somehow it just feels unnatural, and my arm hangs in the air like the slumped over stem of a dead flower.

"How is it okay?" he says, turning on me with a scowl. His face is beet red and for the first time in my life, I am scared of my son.

"I don't know, man," I say, struggling to find the words. "Because... we still have each other, or something?"

He shakes his head at me in disbelief, and says he has to go to the bathroom, shaking my hand from his shoulder with a violent shrug. He doesn't return for a long time, and I am left to my own paranoid thoughts. An elderly couple hobbles their way into the waiting room and sits down across from me. I can hear the old man's raspy breath and wonder how black his lungs are. He's got one of those portable oxygen masks on wheels and his wife keeps clutching at his hands, although it appears that the old man doesn't feel her touch. If I ever get to that point, just throw me off a fucking cliff. Thomas finally returns and sits down a seat away from me. He snatches up one of the magazines from the rectangular table in the middle of the room, glares at me, and starts flipping through the pages. I don't bother trying to say anything more because I've already dug a deep enough hole, so I figure it's better to just stay silent.

As much as I try to fight it, my mind flitters back to the last time I sat in a hospital waiting room. This very same room, in fact, back when mom was on her last legs and could hardly form single word answers to my pathetic and desperate questions; her deflated torso and skeleton limbs, all withered and worn, and me, two short years ago, sitting here feeling sorry for myself and dwelling on my own regrets. Selfish bastard. I remember my father, sitting across from me, eyes on his own feet, tears dripping upon the cold linoleum floor like so many rain drops upon the pavement. I had truly felt sorry for him, back then. Before Ping. He had been a broken man, or at least so I thought, but oh how quickly the heart forgets.

Rebecca Stanfield.

I missed her, perhaps more now than ever. She had been my one confidant; the only person capable of transforming my toxic cynicism into anything remotely positive. It was her way.

"Aren't you mad?" I asked her. This was back when the diagnosis had come back. We were sitting in the living room of their house out in Armprior, my father sitting stone-faced beside my mother on the couch, his hands grasped together in a death grip, staring at the goddamn floor, and me sitting over on the white leather chair across from them, a lump in my throat the size of a fucking boulder.

"What is there to be mad about, Mark?"

"It's... it's just not fair."

She had laughed at me then, a full on cackle, with her head held back and everything.

"My son, surely you've realized by now that life is anything but fair. Life can be a lot of things, but don't you dare expect it to go and treat you special. It's a crapshoot, Mark. Just close your eyes and try to enjoy it!"

"But mom... you're sick. The doc says..."

"I'm not dead yet, Markus," she had said. "Now are we going golfing or what?"

That's how she saw things. Pure. Positive. An infinitely better person than me. She never let her misfortunes get in the way of living her life. And ever since she's been gone, I find myself waking in the night and looking up at the ceiling, attempting to draw on her strength, on her wisdom and sheer lust for life, and time and time again I find myself coming up empty, because I am not capable of capturing her essence; I am not worthy. I missed her more than I can describe. The way she used to smile up at me when I said something snide, shaking her head and tsk-tsk-tsking me. I think she was probably the only person in the world who saw any sort of good in me.

On her deathbed, she refused to be catered to, even though she could barely move. She would wave nurses off who tried to feed her, priests who tried to pray for her, and she died with her head looking up towards the sky, a sort of half smile stretched across her diminished lips. You want to know the last thing she ever said to me? Work hard and be a good person.

I have failed her.

More than I liked to admit.

And then she died. Choking on her own tongue because the disease had robbed her of her motor functions. She was sixty-seven. Plenty of life left in her. And she didn't just slouch around feeling sorry for herself. She had a zest for life. She craved it. And I guess that's the point. Life mocks us. And I can't help but hold every other living person on this planet in contempt, because they are alive and she is not.

I tried reading to her some nights, near the end, when her limbs stopped adhering to the commands of her brain. But I couldn't do it. I'd be sitting there beside her hospital bed, the dim hospital light hanging above, surrounded by foreign beeps and alien noises of the machines which were keeping my mother alive, reading her a Tom Clancy novel (those were her favourites), and I would look up from the page and catch her looking at me with frantic eyes. I could always tell she wanted to say something, because her hand would twitch or her leg would move sporadically, and after looking again into her contorted face, those frantic eyes all bloodshot and beady, the tears would start falling uncontrollably, which would force me to leave the room, her words echoing inside my skull; I'll weep my own bloody tears, thank you very much.

That's why my father could hardly ever visit near the end. He burst into sobs as soon as he entered the room.

I wish I could talk to her.

She was always the only person who could make me see things in a different light. She had the key to my maniacal and cynical mind, and without her, I feel like I'm trapped inside, a prisoner of my own self-doubts.

She wouldn't want to speak with you, Markus. You are a disgrace. An arrogant and selfish man. Blinded by the bright and flashy lights of your own failed ambitions, and the pity you feel for yourself.

She was probably the best damn person I'd ever known. And yet she was dead and here I sit feeling sorry for myself, like in some sort of twisted déjà vu, waiting on the news that my wife has just miscarried in her third trimester. Part of me wants to cry, although there is a voice buried deep inside, where all the black thoughts and sinister ideas come from, who wants me to jump for joy and rejoice.Hallelujiah!

Fuck you.

No, Markus, fuck you.

After another two hours, the doctor finally comes out and summons me with a subtle wave. I take faint notice of the clock hanging in the hallway reading 11:30. My head weighs a hundred pounds upon my neck, and my back aches from the rock-hard waiting room chairs. I can tell by the look on the doctor's face that it's not good, and I see Thomas following me with his eyes as I make my way across the room. It's evident that he can see the bad news coming as well. They might as well have sent out the grim reaper to break the news.

"Mr. Stanfield," he nods. "I'm afraid we've lost the baby. Stillbirth."

I feel a black hole swirling in my stomach, and for a moment I think I might faint. Isn't this what you wanted?

"I'm very sorry."

"Why...." I start, although my voice betrays me, leaving the question hanging in the air like a bad smell.

"Your wife is forty-five, Mr. Stanfield. The risks are always exponentially higher..."

"I know how fucking old my wife is, thank you."

He looks at me with a flash of anger, but I see it pass in an instant, his eyes flickering across my face. "You can go see her shortly," he says quietly. "As soon as they get her cleaned up."

He puts a hand on my shoulder and squeezes, then turns to leave without saying anything else.

"Wait, Doc," I call after him.

He stops and turns back.

"Was it a boy or a girl?"

"It was a girl, Mr. Stanfield."

And then he leaves me to my own desolate thoughts. I turn around but Thomas is no longer in the waiting room, and I can feel my chest tightening. You should be doing summersaults Marky boy, your wish came true.

Wednesday Morning

Driving home from the hospital, I contemplate all that has been laid before me. My daughter is dead. My son hates me. And my wife wants to take a break. It's 12:30am and I haven't slept yet. I am afraid of what I'll see if I close my eyes. The cars stream past me on the highway, mere blurred specs. The moons hangs low in the sky, with an organish tinge. Blood moon.

"Maybe it's a sign," she said, tears staining her splotchy cheeks as I clutched her hands in the cramped hospital treatment room. "I think it might be best if I went and stayed with my mother for a while. Sometime apart might be good for us right now. Besides, my mother needs me, what with her eyes and all."

"What about the boy?"

"I think it would be best if he came with me, Markus. He doesn't seem quite pleased with you at the moment..."

"I didn't mean to offend him..."

"I know you didn't," she said, her eyes like ice. "But that doesn't change the fact you don't seem to know a damn thing about your own family. It's like you don't even care anymore. And I'm not blaming you Markus. It happens. Look at Natalie and Bob, they were trying – but it just wasn't working. Some things just aren't meant to be, you know? I really think a break would be best."

For some reason I said, "But I love you," to which my wife scoffed.

"I want to believe you Markus, I do, but you haven't been proving it. I honestly can't remember the last time you showed me that you loved me. Like really showed me."

"I show it all the fucking time!" I yelled, causing the nurse to

126

poke her mousey little face into the room. One quick look into my eyes sent her squealing back behind the curtains.

"No, you don't. How long have I been asking you to go to the doctor's for a check-up?" and she started crying at this point, somehow talking through her sobs, "but you won't listen to me. You never do. Even over the smallest things."

"What in the Christ does me going to the doctor have anything to do with our situation right now?"

"It's all part of it! And you should know that. You haven't brought me flowers in years, Mark. I can't remember the last time you did something without me having to ask you to do it."

"Am I a fucking mind-reader? Huh? If you want flowers then you should tell me that you want fucking flowers!"

At this point the doctor slipped in through the curtains and reminded me that my wife, whose face was buried in her hands as she sobbed, was very tired and needed some rest. I wanted to slap the glasses right off his face, but I refrained, mostly because I was at a loss as to what I could say to my wife at that point. And you should know that. Why did she have to be so goddamn cryptic all the time. If you want to tell me something... TELL ME!

By the time I pull into the driveway of my empty house, it's just past 1am, and the dark house sits before me all forlorn and foreboding like an opened casket. Thomas elected to go to his grandmother's for the night, and so I was left to my own horrid company.

At least you still have your dog, oh wait...

At least you still have your family, oh wait...

At least you still have...oh wait, Cheryl!

I'm lying in bed with Cheryl at the Minto. She is nuzzled up against my chest, tucked in neatly beneath my arm. Her hair is a sweaty mess and I can see red marks from my fingers around her throat. My lip is sore from her biting it, and I can taste the faintest hint of blood, that metallic sort of taste trickling down the back of my throat. I roll from the bed and make myself a stiff rye and coke while Cheryl tells me about her cheating bastard of a husband. It's 3:30am on Wednesday night, and sleep still seems like a faraway ambition at this point, my head clogged with all sorts of awful and mundane thoughts. Your daughter is dead. Your wife is leaving you. Your son hates you. And you're to blame for every single one of these problems.

"My husband is cheating on me."

"Well, I guess you two have something in common after all!" I say, raising my glass in the air drunkenly. The bottle of rye, which was full not an hour ago, is nearly empty at this point.

"You are the worst person to talk about this stuff with," she says.

"Yes, I certainly am," I say, sipping from my drink and cringing. It's strong.

"I wouldn't care, you know, if he at least pretended to love me when he was at home. The only time we ever talk is when he needs to time out one of his goddamn speeches. It really is all he cares about. Getting into cabinet. You want to know something? He laughed at me when I brought up the idea of having a child. He actually laughed out loud, in my face. And then he came back to me the next day and said, 'you know honey, after thinking it over, it might be good to have a child. It could certainly improve public perceptions...' I got my tubes tied the day after that."

"Does he know that?"

"Of course not."

I start to say something, but then I don't. Your child is dead. I take another pull from my rye and coke, letting the poison fill my head, pushing away all other thoughts, drowning the images of twisted limbs and frozen hearts in a brown wave of intoxication.

"I asked him for a divorce, but he doesn't even love me enough to give me that."

"Why?"

"He says it would look bad. Aesthetically, this could hurt me. Those were his exact words."

"Technically, that's not the proper use of aesthetic..."

"Mark, we need to talk," she says suddenly, sitting up and leaning her back against the wall so that her tits are all poking out and glistening. I can feel my cock getting hard again, but a horrifying thought suddenly thwarts all imminent blood flow.

"Please don't tell me you're pregnant," I say, cringing and biting my tongue. Don't you dare cry in front of her...

"No, it's not that. I'm thinking of leaving my husband."

"Can't say I blame you, when's the last time you two had sex again?"

"This isn't a joke, Markus – I want you to listen to me."

"Okay, I'm listening."

"I think you should leave your wife too."

"Oh, if only life were that simple."

"It could be," she says, raising her eyebrows.

"Cheryl, come on..."

"There's no law against it."

"What are you suggesting Cheryl? That we both leave our significant others, take off down to Mexico and live out the rest of our lives in paradise? I just don't think it would work out that way. Besides, my wife needs me, she's... in pain..."

"You told me just an hour ago about how she said she thinks you two need a break!"

"Yeah, well, it's a traumatic thing to go through... emotions are high. I mean, it's not so simple..."

"And you don't have to exaggerate," she says, "we could just start fresh here, in Canada. You wouldn't have to be far away from your son, and to be honest, from what you've told me about your wife, about the way you treat her, I'm sure she would be better off as well. You don't love her Markus. Why else would you be sitting in this hotel room with me?"

I feel a lump swelling in my throat as my face turns red. She was right, goddamnit. Trace probably would be better off without me. And for some reason, this stirs an inherit will to be a good family man inside me. It'd be like letting Cheryl win if I left. I'd be letting them both win, and somehow this seems absolutely unacceptable to me.

"Do you dream about other women?"

"Pardon?"

"When you're asleep, do you dream about being with other women?"

I look down at Cheryl who is nuzzled against one of the fluffy but utterly disgusting hotel pillows, looking up at me with batted eyelashes, and I suddenly realize what a lost little girl she is, and for the first time in a long time, I genuinely feel sorry for someone.

"Well, I dream about my wife quite often..." I say, not wanting to lead her on.

"Yeah, okay – that makes sense – but do you ever dream about women, other than me and your wife."

And it pains me to admit that I can't remember ever having dreamt about Cheryl, but looking into her glassy eyes, I know I can't possibly tell her that.

"Well..."

"You do, don't you."

"I mean, of course I do," I say, quite puzzled. "I can't control what I dream about."

She sighs.

"Are you actually mad right now?"

"No, of course not," she says. "I was just wondering."

But I can tell, by the way she bats her eye lashes and bites her lower lip, looking away from me over towards the mirror on the hotel wall and staring back at her own reflection, that I've hurt her. She removes herself from the bed and goes over to the window, her naked backside looking silky smooth and tender in the soft light, and standing there with a half-hard cock I realize that no matter how aggressive and domineering she might try to make herself out to be, she couldn't hide her vulnerability from me.

"Do you love me?" she asks, turning her head sideways towards me.

"Cheryl, you were the one who told me this was just for fun – you were the one that assured me nothing more was ever going to come..."

"I know what I said," she snaps, "but I'm asking you a question."

"Cheryl... we're both married."

"Answer me!" she says, almost yelling.

"Fine! No, I don't love you."

And with that, she has seemingly tossed all of her clothes back on in an instant and is swiftly headed for the exit, snatching up her purse from the cushioned chair, and giving me the finger just before she slams the door.

Wednesday Night

It's Wednesday night and I'm sitting all slouched over on the living room couch with my cell phone grasped between my cold fingers. I've managed to convince Trace to come home, at least for now. She has been lying in bed since she got here this afternoon, finally being released from the hospital. We were silent as I rolled her through the parking lot in the hospital wheelchair, an orderly following a few steps behind, just to make sure we didn't abscond with the goddamned thing. Thank you, he said awkwardly after I passed it off to him.

It took considerable effort to drive home, seeing as I had yet to sleep at all from the previous night, and the whiskey was still swimming somewhere down in my stomach. Do you love me? Why were women so consistently crazy? Perhaps you are the crazy one, a voice sneers in my head, for expecting anything different.

My attempts to sooth her are met with ambivalent disregard, leaving me feeling remorseful, guilty, and oddly spiteful (I truly am the most selfish person on the planet). She won't let me rub her back, or her swollen feet. She rejects any food I try to bring her, and our conversations consist of one word answers from her and hollow laughter from my own throat.

Cheryl keeps texting me, and every message that supersedes the previous ignored message becomes progressively more crazy. The most current one in my inbox reads: I'm looking at your wife's Facebook page.

Fantastic.

Tracy hasn't smiled since the hospital, when she told me it was over, and this thought fills me with a sort of melancholy dread that

131

seems to mock me like a frowning clown's mask. I know. I know deep down that I deserve all of this, and yet, somehow, I keep finding ways to feel sorry for myself.

Thomas hasn't spoken to me since the waiting room, and seems content to stay locked up in his bedroom. He's still upset that I wouldn't lend him my car to go see his girlfriend, but of course he knows he can't ask for anything right now.

Essentially, my house is a silent bubble of despair which is slowly driving me insane. I need to get out of here. I need refuge for a night. I punch in some letters and send the text message off to Dick, who responds promptly, saying: see you at the cock.

On my way out the front door I think about calling up to my wife and son to let them know I am leaving, but decide against it in all my cowardly and guilt-ridden shame. They were better off without me here anyways.

Dick gives me a solemn nod as I pull up a bar stool beside him. I take faint notice of his cleanly shaven face and the scent of cologne lingering on his body. He's wearing grey dress pants and a burgundy dress shirt, his suit jacket hung over the back of the bar stool. His forehead beams in the light above the bar.

"I'm sorry," he says, patting a hand on my back as I take my seat. I nod and grimace, staring down at my hands as they rest on the bar counter (they have developed a slight quiver in the past day because of the stress. Either that or its alcohol withdrawal).

"It's a goddamn tragedy..." he continues, but his voice is like an incoherent echo inside my skull. I can barely feed his hand on my back, to be honest; numbed. Every sound I hear is muffled by the constant ringing in my head. This is all your fault.

The bartender tonight is a twenty-something male with tattoos covering his neck and arms, the faded green ink looking as if someone pressed a wet newspaper against his flesh. He's got long hair done up in a man-bun (I hear they are all the rage these days, and somehow, I am sure that my son would have one if he was capable of growing his hair out), and an unkempt beard.

"What can I do for yah, chief?"

"Give me two shots of whiskey and a beer," I tell him, my own voice sounding distant and meek. "Oh, and Dick do you want anything?"

Dick and the bartender share a chuckle, but after studying my cement face they both realize that I am not joking.

"I'll take a shot of whiskey," Dick says sheepishly.

I take a look around the mostly empty bar. A middle-aged woman well past her prime sits alone in a booth, hunched over her glass of red wine with her eyes fixated on her cell phone which is sitting upright on the table. She appears to be mumbling to herself, perhaps willing the phone to ring just so she can participate in some sort of human interaction, even if it comes from a rectangular machine.

There's a young couple sitting at a table near the back, tucked away from the rest of us, and they seem happy enough, their hands clasped together across the table as they look into each other's eyes in that sort of way that only young love can look, causing me to feel a pang of desperate sorrow in the pit of my stomach.

And then I see her...

She's sitting at the table closest to me, her pale flesh glowing in the dim light, hanging grotesquely from her brittle bones. Her mouth is stretched open in a gaping yawn, frozen in a silent scream. Her eyes, all red and glazed over, reaching towards me with her skeleton fingers writhing in the stale air, and I can see that she's choking, my daughter, choking on the air that she was never permitted to breathe.

"Here you are gentlemen," the tattooed bartender says, slamming our shots down on the counter with considerable force, jolting me from my grief driven hallucinations.

"Not sure what your definition of gentlemen is," Dick muses, "cause I'm looking at two middle-aged alcoholic whores!"

Dick and the bartender laugh while I check over my shoulder to see if she's still reaching towards me, but she's gone.

A cold shiver of relief snakes down my spine as I slug back the first shot of whiskey, not waiting for Dick who's holding out his shot in an unmet gesture of cheers. I take a sip of my beer, and then proceed to take the second shot, the whiskey all hot and burning at the back of my throat, momentarily stunning my senses so that for the briefest of seconds, I can forget about the tiny demons dancing on my shoulders, whispering horrifying truths in my ears.

"You okay man?" Dick asks.

"Dick, how's work?" I say, not wanting to address such a meaningless question at the moment. "Help take my mind off all this shit, will yea?"

"Well, we've scrapped the pipeline... for now," he says, grimacing.

"Well shit Dick, I guess you guys are fucked then..."

"While our government is still committed to facilitating and enhancing our natural resources sector, we understand and acknowledge the need for immediate job creation in the West, which is why we've made steps towards allowing for the reopening of several coal generated power plants in Alberta..."

"Are you seriously regurgitating talking points to me right now?"

"Not bad, eh?" he says, nodding his big fat dumb head and grinning. "Wrote em' myself."

"Yes Dick, as far as talking points go, they are bang on. They say a whole lot without really saying anything at all."

"Precisely."

"Aren't the aboriginals and environmentalists going to be upset over the fact that we are reopening coal generated power plants?"

"Meh," Dick shrugs. "Aboriginals and environmentalists are always upset."

I nod and can't help but think he's got a point.

"They're almost as bad as feminists," he says, waving his hand in front of his face before taking a long pull from his pint. He wipes the residue from his lips, burps and pats his belly while I shudder inside to think that this man (and many other men just like him), is in control of our country's decisions and finances.

I take a quick look over my shoulder. She's gone still, although I can sense something in the corner of my eye, hiding over in the corner of the room, a reaching hand perhaps, but I turn back around before I can really focus on it.

"Another shot?" Dick asks.

"Nope, can't do it," I say, chugging what's left of my beer and belching, hammering the empty pint glass on the bar counter. "I'm late for my AA meeting."

On my way to Wilfred Laurier High School I see shadows creeping along the pavement, trailing behind me as I make my demented way down the side streets of downtown Ottawa. The air is moist and salty on this warm spring night. Feels like rain. The sun has set and a bright orange bleeds over the horizon, creeping through the tree tops and buildings to form patches of light on the ground.

I am drunk.

My phone begins ringing in my pocket, and for a fleeting moment I actually hope its Trace so I can finally say all those things I've been meaning to say to her... I'm sorry. I need you. I can still remember the first time we kissed and how it made me feel like floating, and how you used to make my world stop, and I want to feel it again even if I have to work for it because that's what being a man is all about...

But it's not Trace. It's Cheryl.

I let the call go to voice mail.

I take a quick look over my shoulder to ensure that my dead daughter is not following me. The street is empty behind me, and I breathe a sigh of relief.

Walking up the gently rising slope of Lyon Street, past apartment complexes and medium sized houses that cost millions of dollars now strictly because of location, I stumble upon a cardboard box full of discarded books sitting at the edge of a gravel driveway. I stop to inspect some of the books which had been evidently evicted from their homes. William Faulkner's The Sound and the Fury; JP Donleavey's The Ginger Man; Bret Easton Ellis's American Psycho; and Ernest Hemingway's A Farewell to Arms. I am struck with a sudden an unexpected surge of anger. How could anyone in their right mind throw away these books? Each one of them a masterpiece in its own right.

I used to care quite a lot about art (much like politics), but as the years slipped away I suppose most of my passions got put on

135

cruise control. I still read the odd book here and there (mostly non-fiction accounts of semi-celebrities and/or historical figures), but even then, I only picked up every other word. I guess my heart just wasn't in it anymore, as my mother would say.

She had been an avid reader. She also loved to paint. She wasn't going to be selling any of her works for millions of dollars (even now that she was dead), but her paintings were nice all the same. I still had one of her portraits tucked away in the garage. It was a self-portrait she had done when she'd turned fifty-five.

I feel a pang of guilt for the fact that her portrait has been hiding in the garage all this time, and make a mental note to rescue it from the dreary and damp place.

Thinking of her now while I stand on the corner of Lyon and Gilmour clutching these books in my arms, I guess it makes me feel sort of rotten, considering I'm about as angry and bitter as any one man can be. I check my watch and see that I have to keep moving if I want to make it to the meeting. I stuff the Hemingway novel in my back pocket and continue my slow ascent towards the school.

I get to the school twenty minutes late and make sure to wash my mouth out with water in the bathroom before entering the gymnasium. I come through the back doors and make quite a racket in the process, the heavy door slamming behind me, and lots of heads turn aggressively towards me with narrowed eyes. I search for a friendly face as I approach the rows of chairs, but I fail to find Jim in the group.

I take a seat in the back row just as a cleanly shaven and well-dressed man approaches the microphone. He looks more out of place here than I do, and I shuffle forward a bit in my seat, suddenly quite interested to hear what this stranger has to say. I take faint notice that Jim does not appear to be here.

"Hello," the man says, "my name is Jason."

"Hi Jason," a chorus of people respond in unison.

"This is my first time here..." he pauses, looking down briefly. "I've... struggled this past year, made some mistakes – some pretty big mistakes. I guess... well I guess I sort of ruined my life."

"There's always another chance!" someone yells out.

Jason nods absently before continuing; "Yes, well I hope so anyways. This time last year I was running my own business. I had four employees and our company was profitable, we were actually looking to hire more people. You see, we developed a program for private Real Estate training so people could sell and buy their own houses. It was a hit, especially with the recession and all, everyone wanted to save money.

"Things got bad about six months ago, when our patent expired and dozens of copycat programs hit the web. Soon enough, there was a free version that you could download, and well, that was the beginning of the end. Our sales pretty much fell off the charts. That's when I started drinking, heavily. I would wake up in the morning without knowing what to do, or where to turn... I figured it would pass, that I was just having a rough year – but last week I woke up in the hospital with a broken nose, cracked rib, and a gash on the back of my head. I still have no recollection of what happened..."

At this point, Jason breaks down, not weeping, but he turns his head away from us and quickly swipes at his eyes with the backs of his hands.

"I'm not sure if things would have turned out any differently, with or without the booze, but I just declared bankruptcy last month, and the business is now closed."

The room in silence for a moment. Someone coughs and I can hear myself breathing, which is distressing to me. You sound drunk.

"Well, I think that's all I have to say for now, thank you for letting me share with you all today."

Various people shout out their last calls of encouragement as Jason takes a seat near the front.

"Is there anyone else who would like to share?"

The room stands quiet.

For a moment, I almost rise from my seat. It's time, I think to myself.

And then suddenly, an unexpected burst of air comes catapulting from my throat, culminating in a loud belch that echoes off the walls of the gymnasium.

Heads are turned and then shaken. A couple people cough

137

awkwardly. The man at the microphone stares back at me with a half-opened mouth and I can feel my face growing red. Whatever, who gives a shit? I can smell the booze wafting from my mouth in a hot gust.

I sit back down.

After what seems like minutes, some woman gets up and heads to the microphone to share her story. Single mother, deadbeat ex-husband who has trouble keeping up with the monthly child support payments, dead-end job, struggling with debt, you know, the typical pitiful story of another lost soul bathing in all the glory and glamour of the new-aged middle class.

Twenty minutes go by and the meeting is adjourned, my fellow addicts and I moving together like a herd of lost cattle. I can feel my buzz wearing off and this troubles me. I head over to the back corner of the room to get some coffee. There's a couple people I recognize mingling about the gymnasium, and they give me subtle nods as I pass by, the polished wooden floor gleaming in the incandescent light, making me squint a little.

I probably looked quite inebriated, to be honest.

I pour myself a coffee and start gulping it back black. The bitter taste hits my tongue and throat like a hot wave, giving me that instant sensation of momentary energy. Such fleeting moments of this life based upon our previous experiences, the same rush, the same buzz; we are always attempting to recapture the same feelings we've had before, and yet somehow, those original sensations, those initial instances of experience remain elusive (much like my sobriety), and we spend most of our lives trying to relive our past in one way or another.

I pull out the Hemmingway novel and start flipping through the pages. I had read A Farewell to Arms before, and a comforting thought surfaces in my mind: if Hemmingway could write such beautiful words then surely being an alcoholic can't be all bad, I mean, the guy was a genius and he was drunk before noon on most days.

The comforting rationalizations of an alcoholic (that would be a good title for this novel!).

I scan the room again and confirm that Jim is not here. I approach one of the familiar looking men in the room and ask if he's seen Jim today.

"Oh, Jimmy boy. Yeah, good question. Haven't seen him. I think Todd is his sponsor, maybe you should ask him."

"And Todd is..." I ask, realizing just how little I knew about my fellow alcoholics (I've never been big on community spirit).

The man points out Todd and I go over to him, repeating the same question.

"Oh," the man says, gulping and looking down at his shoes. "Jim's... well, I don't think he's well. I tried calling him several times today, he answered once and I could hear the booze in his voice. He said something about his daughter and hung up. I'm worried."

"Oh gee," I say. "That sounds... unfortunate."

The man nods gravely and turns away from me.

I watch him walk off, shuffling his feet like a disheartened zombie. I take a look at the clock on the wall and see that it's past 10:00pm, and so I make my way towards the door. I find myself wondering about Jim, and hoping that he's okay. Probably just sick or something. But in my heart I can feel that there's something wrong. A sort of alcoholic telepathy speaks to me through the air, and I feel a fleeting sort of urgency that causes me to become anxious and nervous, that sort of tingling beneath your skin, and the way my heart starts beating. I hope he's okay.

I'd worry about yourself, the sinister voice in the back of my head pipes in. You're the one who just showed up shit-hammered to a goddamn AA meeting.

Shut-up.

No, you shut-up.

Sometimes, I hated myself. I truly did. You can be a real asshole.

Thursday

It's Thursday night and after spending the entire day attempting to pull Trace from our bed, and failing, I have relapsed (despite my best intentions). I am seated across form Cheryl, both of us half-naked, in a hotel room at the Minto Suites. We ordered room service, and I have for the most part devoured my steak while Cheryl continues to pick and prod at her fish.

"I don't know if I can keep doing this," I say suddenly, the words tumbling from my mouth in a torrent of hot shame.

"Doing what?"

"Betraying the people I love," I say, staring out the window towards the river.

"Oh please," she scoffs, taking a long gulp from her wine. She has her hair up in a bun and she's wearing one of the hotel nightgowns without bothering to do it up at the front. Her tits are threatening to poke out from beneath the silky fabric, and I can't help but study her areolas as I chew on my overcooked steak. "Now that the baby is... gone, you can leave her. You should leave her and be with me, Mark. Like we always talked about."

My eyes shake in their sockets as I glare back at her.

"Haven't you been hoping for this? Isn't this what you've been hoping for the past six months?"

"I think we need to take a break."

She looks back at me, her mouth slightly ajar.

"You're kidding."

"Afraid not."

"Look, I know you're going through a rough time, Mark. I get it. But listen to me, you were miserable. You were wishing for

140

this to happen. You're the one who told me you don't love her anymore. That you find her disgusting and annoying..."

"Cheryl," I say through clenched teeth. "If you insinuate once more that I have been wishing for my unborn daughter to die..."

Her eyes bulge as her face flushes. "Okay, okay Markus. I can tell that you're upset. Let's not get into it..."

"I'm serious, it's over."

"What about me?"

"Huh?" I say, not really hearing her as I continue staring out the window.

"I said, what about me - don't you love me?"

"Come on Cheryl, we both know what this was."

"Was?"

"Yes, was."

She throws the glass with remarkable accuracy, and surprising force, and when it shatters on my forehead I see a bright flash of light, and while I'm seeing stars I have to dodge the plate, which shatters on the wall behind me. She could be a real peach sometimes...

"You piece of shit, you limp-dicked piece of fucking shit."

"Hey that was only once..."

"Shut-up!" she screams at me, standing from her chair with such force that it falls over backwards.

"...because I drank too much rye..."

"FUCK YOU!"

"Okay, okay, just calm down for a second..."

"You think I'm just going to let you dump me? Drop me off like some fucking secretary whore. I make more money than you, I know more people than you. And under normal circumstances, a guy who looks like you would never get to fuck a girl like me."

"What about this seems normal to you?" I ask, a napkin pressed tightly against my forehead. I can feel the bump already swelling, and the napkin comes back with blood on it when I remove it from my head.

"You know what, Jack?" she says, getting up from her chair and moving over towards her clothes hung hastily on the dresser.

141

"You're a monster. Somehow, you've convinced yourself that you're a loving husband, a caring father, a passionate man, but you're just pretending. You're just pretending right now because it feels good, but a year from now you'll be fucking some other gullible girl, and your faggot son will be humping some guys ass..."

"Hey now, he's not gay, apparently..."

"How are you still making jokes? Can't you see that I hate you, are you forgetting what I'm capable of?"

This time I can't think of anything witty to say, and I watch the spark of victory flicker in her eyes, like a can of gasoline has just been ignited behind them, and she takes a step back towards me, and then another one.

"I'll tell your wife," she says with a crooked smile. "You know I have pictures."

"Well... so do I..."

"Go ahead, show my husband - he'll kick your ass and I'll still get the house."

"Cheryl, come on..."

"You're a filthy old man with a small prick."

"So, haven't I suffered enough?"

"No," she says, "no, not nearly enough."

And with that, she scoops up her jacket and slips out the door, letting it shut softly behind her. Why is it that every time I try to do the right thing, it backfires in my fucking face? It takes me a moment to notice that I have a hard on after all that arguing, and this of course causes me to laugh as blood continues to leak from my forehead.

"What's happened to your head?"

I am taken aback seeing my wife out of bed as I walk in through the front door. She is standing in the front hallway wearing her cotton nightgown with a coffee in her hand.

"You should see the other guy," I say. "It's good to see you out of bed."

"I couldn't stand lying there anymore," she sighs. "I've been writing for the past two hours. The words are really pouring out..."

142

"That's good, baby."

"I've missed you," she says. "And I'm sorry I was so hard on you after..."

"It's okay," I tell her. "I know how hard this has been. And... I'm sorry too, for everything."

And like a scene out of a bad romance movie, we embrace each other in the hallway, her arms wrapping around my neck and squeezing tight. I can feel some of the coffee spilling down my back, and even though it's pretty fucking hot (not to mention the fact that this is a new shirt), I don't give a shit. I can feel her breasts against me as I squeeze her back and I kiss her neck, sucking hard on the flesh that once made me so excited. She sticks her tongue in my ear and whispers, 'I want to fuck you.'

"What about Thomas?" I say in quick breaths.

"He's gone, took the train to Kingston to see Alisha."

"I think it's Ayisha?"

"Whatever!" she says, fiddling with the zipper on my pants.

We pile into her closet of an office and I've got her perched up on the desk with her legs spread, the nightgown now completely open revealing her naked torso. She smells like coconut and I can feel her heart beating rapidly inside her chest. Her breasts are heaving and gleaming with sweat and I can feel my dick getting hard... and then I make the fatal mistake of looking at her vagina.

It's a goddamn train wreck. It looks like a bombed out rebel village in Syria.

Suddenly, Tracey starts laughing.

"What?" I say.

"You should see your face," she says gasping, "you looked like you just walked in on a murder scene."

"Pretty much," I say grimacing. "I don't think we should..."

"No, of course not. It hurts to pee for Chrissake."

"Hm, well," I say, looking down at the bulge in my pants.

"Seems to be a slight protuberance here," Trace says, gripping my cock in her hand. She smiles up at me in a very sexy way, and for a fleeting moment, I suddenly remember why I fell in love with her in the first place.

She takes me in her mouth and it's warm, so warm, and despite her lack of practice, she performs amicably, stroking and sucking, her tongue like an electric worm, and I reach down and start playing with her tits while she performs the long-lost art of fellatio like a seasoned pro.

And after it's all over, she wipes her mouth and kisses me on the cheek. "I need a fucking drink," she says.

So, we go to the kitchen and pour ourselves a couple glasses of white wine. Her cheeks are glowing all red and rosy, and I catch her smiling at me in a way I have not seen in some time. We sit at the kitchen table and after finishing our first glasses in record time, we pour ourselves another.

"Ah," my wife says, smacking her lips. "Tastes so good. It's been a long eight months without getting drunk."

"I don't get drunk," I say, "I get even."

"Oh shush," she says, laughing. "I miss this."

"Me too."

And we smile at each other in the bright light, momentarily forgetting all the hardship and stress, the realities of our utterly mediocre middle-aged lives, and I can feel my heart swell in a way that hasn't happened in years. That bump-bump-bump in my chest.

"I'm sorry, Trace..."

"It's okay," she says, "it's not your fault."

"I keep thinking about what it would have been like to have a daughter, a little girl... and despite how scared I was... I think I would have liked it."

"You would have been a good father," she says, tears welling in her eyes. "You would have been great."

I get up from the chair and go over to her, wrapping my arms around her from behind and squeezing. I can feel her heart beat through her chest, and it sounds like the saddest song I've ever heard. I scoop her up as best I can from the chair (there once was a time when I could actually pick her up and carry her up the stairs, back when I was stronger and she was lighter). Together we go upstairs and undress. We climb into bed and hide together under the covers like we used to. I kiss her neck and run my hand down her back. I wish your pussy wasn't obliterated, I whisper in her ear, because I would go to town on that thing right now. This makes her laugh and cringe and hit me on the chest with her fist.

"You're so nasty," she says.

"You love it."

"I do."

We lie in silence for a bit, staring at each other, at the ceiling, at the wall. It was soothing, just soaking each other's company up like a dry sponge.

"I had to delete the Facebook account today," she says quietly. "It made me cry."

For a moment I think she's talking about her own account, but then I realize she means the one that she made for the baby. Ol' ? Stanfield. Thinking about that question mark sends an uncomfortable shiver down my spine.

"What would we have named her?" I ask.

"Well... I was thinking Rebecca. After your mother."

In those few simple words, she has effectively melted my heart. I grab her and squeeze her and kiss her rapidly on the neck and cheek and lips.

We lie in beautiful silence again for a while.

"I feel like I don't know you anymore, Mark. We used to talk about everything, tell each other everything... about work, about our dreams, what we had to eat that day... I used to love knowing all those things about you."

"I remember," I nod, staring into her brown eyes.

"Why did we stop?"

"Oh god, I don't know, Trace..."

"Do you remember when Thomas was born?" she asks, turning to me with widened eyes.

"Of course I do."

"He was so loud... so upset... and you held him in your arms and looked at me with the most horrified face I've ever seen on a man. It was adorable. And we smiled at each other, and in that instant, he stopped crying..."

"Are you sure you're remembering that right?"

"Does it matter?"

"I guess not."

"God, we would have been right up against it with another kid. I hadn't even thought about that..." she says, her head propped up at an angel against the palm of her hand. "Markus, are we in trouble, financially?" she asks all wide eyed.

"Yes."

"Is it bad?"

"Not so bad..."

"Markus, I want us to stop lying to each other. I don't want to keep living in a house of half-truths and things left unsaid. I want you to be able to confide in me. That's how this whole marriage thing is supposed to work, you know? We are supposed to help each other, rely on each other. And more than anything else, Mark, I want to trust you again."

"We are okay, Trace. I promise," I say through a strained jaw. The pile of discarded bills sitting in the trunk of my car surfaces in my mind like a perverted thought, and I look Trace in the eyes and tell her I love her, hoping beyond hope that I actually mean it.

"You've got a freckle on your back that should probably be looked at Markus."

"Jesus," I say. "Why do you have to say stuff like that?"

"Because! You refuse to go to the doctors. I'm not trying to scare you. You do that to yourself."

"Well, it's tough not to get scared when you're constantly being reminded of all the different ways you could be dying."

"Most people talk about these sorts of things, Markus. It's normal..."

Most people are idiots.

"...and most people go to the doctor's office on a regular basis," she adds.

"Yeah, okay - I get it. I'll call Doctor Von Heyman tomorrow."

"Good," my wife smiles triumphantly.

And she kisses me then, on the cheek, and for a moment I wonder if perhaps things might work out okay. If maybe, just maybe, we could get over this hump and come out stronger on the other side. Stranger things have happened, no? These sorts of stories are always being told, a couple goes through a traumatic event, and boom, after some trials and tribulations, they come out of it better off than when they started! And I let these whimsical and delusional thoughts fill my head like a leaking gas line, because what the hell? Maybe that was half my problem. Maybe it was time to get positive! Optimism is contagious they say, or at least, I think they say that. Whatever. I'll fucking say it then.

Friday

I'm sitting in my office with my shoes off staring blankly at my computer screen wondering how many people waste their entire fucking lives sitting in uncomfortable high-backed rotatable chairs with wheels staring at the goddamn glow of the computer screen while the radiation from the computer slowly microwaves their brains (not to mention their genitals). I can picture a world of pale-skinned creatures stumbling around the streets, a bunch of socially awkward, impotent mother fuckers who can't remember how to make love, but can type over one hundred words a minute and have over one thousand friends on Facebook.

I've tried calling the Scholaces three times today, and have yet to hear back from them. I have a sneaking suspicion that they are backing out... which is fine with me because it will allow me to finally drop them as clients. Forget the computers, the thought of enduring another house showing with the lovely couple is enough to make me impotent.

I have a doctor's appointment this afternoon, finally, and I can't stop poking and prodding at my testicles (not in the usual manner of which I poke and prod, mind you), checking for any unusual lumps or protuberances, and I keep finding what I think are little balls of cancer, although I can't be sure because my ball-sac is so wrinkled and loose it's hard to tell where the flesh ends and the balls begin.

Regardless, I've managed to convince myself that I certainly have some form of cancer and am likely on my last legs of life.

You see what going to the doctor does to me?

My phone vibrates against the desk and I scoop it up, hoping it's the Scholaces, but it's just a text message from Dick wanting to go for lunch beers. I sigh and toss my phone back onto the desk with the indifference of a teenager who has just been asked about the state of the economy. There is no part of me that wants to listen to whatever trivial and redundant issue that Dick was currently consumed by. Fucking politicians. Somehow they always succeeded in convincing themselves that whatever issue they were focusing on was the only issue that mattered.

You could go for a beer though...

My phone starts buzzing again and I scoop it up, answering it right away once I see that it's my magnificent clients.

"Hello Mr. and Mrs. Scholace!"

"Hello," they say in unison, like well-trained conjoined twins.

"We need to have a discussion, Mr. Stanfield."

"That's what phones are usually used for," I say, unable to control myself. I can feel it coming already, like a bad break-up. "What can I help you with today?"

"Well that's the thing," Mrs. Scholace says.

"We no longer need your help with anything..." finishes Mr. Scholace.

"I see... well, um... I'm sorry to hear that. I would be remised if I failed to remind the two of you about the client contract you signed with me back when we started this whole process..."

"Ah yes, the contract," Mrs. Scholaces starts.

"We've had our lawyer take a look at it..." Mr. Scholace adds.

"And he's assured us that any obligations, financial or otherwise, that are contained within said contract..."

"Are unconstitutional and violate our rights as consumers, so... this contract is..."

"Null and void."

Fucking lawyers.

"May I ask just what changed your mind? Are you two simply not in the market anymore or...?"

"Oh no, we are still quite in the market."

"In fact, our cousin Morty has just made an offer that he is quite confident will be accepted by the opposing parties."

"We are very excited," pipes in Mrs. Scholace.

"Your cousin Morty, eh? Well... that's fucking fantastic."

"There's no need for profanity, Mr. Stanfield."

"You're absolutely fucking right," I respond. "There is certainly no need for it. However, I was certainly in dire need of this deal, and since you two bumbling, inconsolable morons seem intent on fucking me over, I guess you could say these two needs sort of balance each other out, wouldn't you agree?"

"Good-bye, Mr. Stanfield."

"Good-bye, you fucking assholes."

On my way to Doctor Von Haymen's office, I wonder if perhaps I could have handled the whole Scholace situation differently (like a professional adult, for instance?). But fuck that. Those simple-minded bastards. They had pulled the oldest trick in the book. Hire some poor-sap independent agent who lacks the legal backing of an entire realtor company such as Royal Lepage, get that poor-sap to show you dozens of homes, quoting you prices and showcasing various neighborhoods, then, once you've decided just exactly what you're looking for, fire that poor-sap and get a close friend or relative to close the deal with minimum commission.

And Presto! You are now a proud home owner (meanwhile, I am about one month away from being foreclosed on).

But, as often happens in this life, an unfortunate event seems to be counter balanced by a fortunate one, and I can't help but think about last night with Trace. We seemed together again, for the first time in a long time, and I am shocked (and almost appalled) at the realization that I am actually excited to get home and see her.

I pull into the crowded hospital parking lot and the usual sense of foreboding that accompanies me upon my approach to those automatic sliding doors at the front entrance of Ottawa General seems to have abandoned me. May as well get this over with...

The smell of antibacterial spray and antiseptic wafts through the air as the fluorescent lights gleam upon the polished linoleum floors, the light bouncing back up so that it makes me squint. I wonder if they colour the floors puke green in order to camouflage actual vomit? I find myself a seat in the corner of the waiting room and sit anxiously on the edge, surveying my fellow patients through squinted eyes. There's an elderly couple sitting together, their wrinkled hands clasped between the seats. The wife looks calmly on while the husband fidgets. It appears clear who is here to see the doctor. I felt bad for the old man, already he looked lost. They say when a spouse dies, it won't be long until the remaining one follows their partner into the afterlife, and for once in my life I can see the appeal and beauty of such a fact (up until yesterday, I always assumed my spouse would be the cause of my death).

There's a mother with her young daughter sitting across from me, which fills me with a sour regret that lingers in the pit of my stomach. I will never know that feeling. I will never know what it's like to wait with my daughter in the hospital because my daughter is dead. The shock and despair of it all was still settling in my system. In fact, I can hardly remember my wife being pregnant. It's as if the past seven months were a dream.

I shift in my seat and I can feel a slight pain in my groin. I discreetly brush my hand down there and wonder if the bump I'm feeling is natural or some sort of mutated tumor. Regardless, I would face it together, with my loving wife and family, and in that moment, I felt truly empowered. Fearless. A loving husband has nothing to fear but the loss of his wife!

And then I see her...

She's sitting at the far end of the room, her skin pale as milk, but her eyes are blood red. Heavy black circles surround her sockets and her gaunt face hangs from her skull in misshapen clumps. She has the appearance of a teenager; however her size is that of a two year old child, all dwarfed and hunched over. Her dark hair is damp and stringy, hanging from her head like wet strands of cotton, and her mouth is moving, although no sound can be heard. She is staring right at me. Her feet dangle from the chair as her legs are too short to reach the floor. Suddenly she hops down from her seat and begins shuffling over towards me in these horrid short steps, staggering and frantic.

A gasp escapes my throat, drawing the attention of the others

151

in the waiting room. I try to keep my composure as my dead daughter's mouth widens into a gaping black hole. I watch as long legged insects begin to crawl from her mouth, their legs reaching and pulling at the sides of her lips, and they scamper down her arms and legs onto the floor, scurrying towards me with their black furry bodies.

You did this, a voice whispers in my head.

Don't you love me daddy?

Won't you tuck me in at night?

Won't you protect me from all the boys?

I squeeze my eyelids shut and rub at them frantically, but, much to my horror, I find her standing right in front of me upon reopening them. Her eyes have turned black and I can see my horrified reflection staring back at me through her dead pupils.

I'm a little slut daddy. I love cock. I want to fuck. I want to be a pornstar and make movies on the internet and would you eat my ass if I asked you too, daddy? Ohhhhh yes, please, I like it...

At this point I have both my feet pulled up to my chest and I am hyperventilating.

When the nurse taps me on the shoulder I nearly shit myself.

"AH!" I scream out, jolting to my feet.

"Sir, Mr. Stanfield, are you okay?" She is a hefty woman with red frizzy hair that's done up in a lazy bun, sitting atop her head like a bird's nest. Her uniform is wrinkled and hangs from her body like loose flesh.

"I... errr," I look around the room, but she's gone. Vanished into thin air.

"We've been calling your name. Did you not hear us?"

"I must have been... I sort of dozed off I guess..."

"Well," the nurse says, her eyes narrowing as she looks me over, "you're up. Doctor Von Heyman will see you now."

I say thank-you and hustle from the waiting room. Curious eyes follow me from the room and I can't help but wonder if I've actually died and gone to Hell. I suppose it wouldn't be surprising if Hell turned out to be a hospital waiting room. In fact, that would make a whole helluva lot a sense, if you ask me.

152

Cancer...

In my balls...

I'm sitting in my car in the hospital parking lot, my mind numb and feeling an empty sort of sorrow digging its way deeper into my stomach.

There's a protrusion present. We'll want to do some more tests, and certainly we will need to take a blood sample before you leave today. There's no need to worry, at least not yet...

Yeah, easy for you to say, Doc.

I start to look up the odds of survival on my phone but wimp out before the Google page loads. I can feel a tingling rush moving through my body and it feels as if my life is replaying in front of my eyes in slow motion. My childhood, spent outside, playing with sticks and dirt and hoses like young boys used to do. Playing road hockey. Playing basketball. My first kiss. Shirley from my grade 8 class who had developed quickly and whose boobs I tried to touch but she whispered No. The daunting hallways of my high school, resonating a feeling of resentment and regret deep within me; wasted years! Years spent trying to be cool, or popular, or get laid. Has anything really changed? My marriage. Tracey. My son. Gay? Apparently not. Do I even know him? Wasted fucking years.

I speed up, driving like a maniac down the one-way streets of Ottawa, up Bay, onto Gladstone, over to Bronson, weaving in and out of the traffic like a madman. People honk their horns but I am deaf to them. There's a little girl walking with her mother, and they are holding hands and for some reason this makes me burst into tears. I see a man in a wheelchair struggling to get over the curb and I begin to sob uncontrollably, the road a blackish blur in front of me.

For the first time in years, all I want is my wife. I want to hold her, for her to hold me. Rub my head and tell me everything is going to be okay.

We will study your charts carefully and consult with our specialists, but please be prepared for surgery. A phone call will be coming soon, and it is imperative that we tackle this head on.

With some diligence and a little luck, we should be able to beat this thing.

So much uncertainty, clouding my mind like marijuana fog. I wish I could smoke a fucking jay right now.

After what seems like hours, my mind slowly torturing me, imploding on itself in anxiety and fear and regret and guilt, pretty much every negative goddamn emotion you can think of, I finally pull into the driveway of my home and lurch up the steps to my front door, swinging it open in tremendous fashion, tears staining my cheeks like fresh rain, and there's an emptiness to the house, I can sense it. Fuck. She's not home. The one time in a decade when I really, truly wanted to see Trace... Why? Why was life such a cruel and fickle bitch?

There's a flicker in the living room and my heart lifts.

I rush into the living room but to no avail. It is empty, except for the laptop sitting open on the coffee table, a low hum filling my ears. I can see Tracey's Facebook page has been left open and this strikes me as odd, seeing how protective she had grown with her goddamn Facebook. I approach the coffee table and my eyes widen in horror.

There is a conversation window left open, and I can make out images sitting there all stagnant in the chat convo, too small yet to make out exactly what... I look at the top of the chat window and let out an audible gasp. Cheryl Price. My wife has been talking to Cheryl. I look at the chat window and see pictures of myself, naked, holding my pathetic erect dick in my hands, standing there in all the glory of adultery and impropriety. I scroll through the chat and see more pictures of myself, pictures of Cheryl, also naked.

That fucking bitch...

I feel a twist in my stomach and run to the kitchen sink, spraying vomit all over the faucet and tiled wall behind, chunks of today's ham sandwich and cheese staining the steel sink. I cough and spit out the remains, tears welling in my eyes. What have I done?

I turn around to find a note sitting on the kitchen table.

I pick it up between trembling fingers.

Markus,

I am gone. Cheryl told me everything. She seems like QUITE
THE LOVELY LITTLE WHORE. I hope it was worth it. I'm
going to my mother's house. Please don't call.

-T

It takes me a moment to realize that Trace has left this little
message on an Eviction Notice from the bank, which demands
full payment within thirty days. My wife has left another message
beneath this which reads: Why didn't you tell me we were fucked?
    Defeated, I collapse in one of the wooden chairs surrounding
the kitchen table, holding my head in my hands and feeling a
slight ache coming from my testicles. So, this is it. This is how
it's going to end. Alone. Cancer. Cuckolded. It's even worse than I
could have ever imagined. Outside rain begins to fall, and I guess
that suits the situation just fine. I wonder if there's any fucking
beer in the fridge...

Saturday

I awake the next morning on the couch with a dry mouth and a sore back, my legs spilling over the armrest, and for a moment I think I can smell Trace cooking breakfast from the kitchen, but upon closer inspection I realize it is simply the socks on my feet which smell like rotten eggs. I check my phone to see if Trace has messaged me, but there's nothing. Radio silence.

She seems like QUITE THE LOVELY WHORE!

What have I done?

The day sits before me like an open sore. I want to bury myself. Cover me in dirt and see if maybe I grow back as a better man.

Daddy?

I jolt up from the couch, twirling around towards the direction of the voice. And there she is, standing all hunched over with her black hair covering her pale face, she is pointing at me with skeleton fingers, her entire body shaking, convulsing, and I can see white foam coming from her mouth, bubbling from the corners of her lips like soap suds.

Look what you've done daddy. You're all alone now. There's no one left. You've destroyed us all. You filthy old man. Couldn't keep your dick in your pants, eh? You slut. Whore.

"Please, stop..."

Do you want to fuck me too, daddy? I can spread my legs if you want me too...

At this point, blood starts to pour from between her legs in a grotesque torrent and I am forced to run from the living room and into the kitchen. But she's waiting for me by the fridge, her thin lips pulled back in a cruel grin, and those eyes, those red-black eyes which remain fixated upon me. She cackles then, a harsh and horrible sound that fills me with dread. I retreat from the kitchen, dashing through the living room and out into the front foyer. I make it out the front door, not bothering to stop and put on my shoes, and I rush to my car where I slam the door behind me and sit there in the driver's seat, my hands clasped tightly around the steering wheel, my breath rattling in my chest.

Am I going crazy?

Without really knowing where I am going, I start the car and pull out of the driveway, speeding down the street, past the neighbours for whom I know nothing about. There's a clicking inside my head like the second hand of a clock.

I come to an abrupt halt at a stop sign and wait for a woman with a baby carriage to cross, taking her time as most mothers with children are apt to do. I take a deep breath and try to relax, but it's at this point that my dead daughter's head comes popping up from the woman's carriage, and she snarls at me revealing a set of pointy teeth. The white foam is bubbling from her mouth again, and she starts to laugh, inaudible to the woman with the carriage, but I can hear it, inside my head, like an insect caught inside my skull, scratching, itching, AHHHHHHH!

My tires squeal as I speed away, barely waiting for the woman to make it across the street. She gives me a contorted look and shakes her head. If only she knew the demons which had made my conscience their home.

After driving around aimlessly for some time, I stop at the LCBO and purchase a 26er of rye, Forty Creek, of course, the finest of the cheapest whiskies. And despite the odd looks from the clerks towards my shoeless feet, they sold me the damn booze anyways as I rambled on about ghosts and regrets...

Oh, if only Jim could see me now!

Thinking of Jim sends a pang of guilt through my spine, and I wonder if the old boy is doing okay...

Before I can really comprehend or realize it, I find myself parked out front of Jim's apartment (he had dragged me here once after a particularly despicable display I put on during one of our

AA meetings, which involved a broken bottle, more than a touch of vomit, and some abusive language). It was a rundown building on the Westside, off Carling, the bricks all brown and worn, and those tiny windows that some apartment buildings have which gave off the appearance of a prison. All they needed were bars on the windows.

I get out of my car and quickly check my surroundings. No sign of my daughter. Good. I can feel my heart rate slow and the hairs on my neck finally settle. The air smells of summer, that scent of foliage and sunshine and heat. The sun ducks behind a wall of clouds as I make my way across the street. As I'm trying to look up Jim's buzzer, an older woman exits the building, and since I know which apartment he lives in, I slip in behind her and head on up to the third floor.

In the hallway, it smells distinctly of cigarettes. That combined with the typical moldy smell of such buildings made breathing almost unbearable. I quickly scuttle towards room 333 and rap my knuckles against the old wooden door. Much to my surprise, the door swings open. Apparently ol' Jim hadn't quite managed to shut it all the way, which worries me.

"Hey, Jim?" I call out.

Nothing.

I move inside the apartment and am struck with an overwhelming stench of booze, cigarettes, and something that very much resembles urine. There's a stack of empty beer cases by the door and two sets of badly worn dress shoes. The kitchen sits before me perpendicular to the front door, and to my right is the living room. I can see in the kitchen that the sink is over flowing with dirty dishes, and there appears to be a white powdered substance laying atop the kitchen counter, along with a few empty liquor bottles.

Oh Jim, what have you been up to?

I hear a grunt and what sounds like someone trying to roll over or perhaps stand up. I enter the living room and find Jim sprawled out on his couch, the lower half of his body spilling off the cushions and his arms flung back behind his head. His pupils are rolled back revealing the whites of his eyeballs, and he's got

158

a considerable amount of drool clinging to his cheek, a pool of it is visible upon the fabric beside his bald head. The clothes he's wearing look as if they haven't seen a laundry machine in some time, and I can see that he has pissed himself, which explained the smell...

Dim blue light bleeds through the apartment window, casting everything in a grey sort of tinge.

His living room is sparse, there's a cheap black table from IKEA with a medium sized flat screen television sitting on it, dust coating the table and base of the TV. He has a matching coffee table and I can see more white residue scattered on the surface (and it is most certainly not dust). Tsk tsk tsk. Alcohol was a hard-enough addiction to shake, but coke was a whole other level. I had dabbled with the devil's dandruff back in my younger and more venerable days, when I worked on Parliament Hill (that shit was rampant on the Hill, politicians made for horrible drug addicts).

I gently nudge Jim's shoulder. "Hey buddy," I say. "Wake up big man."

"Fuck-you wah?" he mumbles.

"I want you to get up and talk to me, Jim. It's me, Markus."

"Markus..." he says, breathing deeply. "He drinks too much."

"Yes," I say. "Yes, he certainly does. I didn't see you at the meeting on Wednesday..."

Finally, Jim gathers the strength and composure to pull himself up. His face has a yellowish tinge to it and there are tiny red bumps all along the edges of his lips and nostrils. He opens his eyes and rubs at them, blinking like a new born bird who has never seen the sun before. It made for quite an ugly site, to be honest. I watch him survey the scene, looking at me momentarily and then down at the coffee table. He scoops up the credit card sitting idly on its surface and chalks up the remaining coke into a long thin line, which he then proceeds to snort loudly, his nose sounding like a broken garburator.

He exhales deeply as if he's just found tranquility, and lights up a smoke. Meanwhile, I stand there awkwardly wondering just what in the hell it says in the AA sponsor handbook for this type of situation? If you happen to find your sponsee lying in his own filth surrounded by empty bottles, cigarette butts, and cocaine, please be sure to open a window and offer to help him change from his soiled pants. Do not attempt moving if unconscious, as this could lead to confrontation or contamination. And if there happens to be an extra line, go ahead and snort that shit up, because Lord knows you could probably use the pick-me-up.

"Sorry you have to see me like this," he says finally, staring out the living room window.

"What the hell happened?" I ask him.

"I dunno," he sighs. "Nothing really, I guess. That's the problem."

"What do you mean?"

"Well, I stopped by my daughter's place, you know, to see the baby, but she wouldn't let me inside. And that was fine, I mean, it's not like I really expected her to let me in, considering last time I was in her house I ended up stealing her purse..."

"Jesus Jim, I never knew..."

"Yeah, I hide it well," he shrugs, his pupils like tiny pencil points. "But anyways, because of that, I had a drink. And then because I had a drink, I had another, which made me feel guilty as all hell, so then I had another. Then I ordered an eight-ball of coke, and before I knew it, five days had gone by. Five fucking days, and I can't remember shit. Five wasted days, and I haven't been to work. For all I know, I've been terminated, which is more than I deserve."

"Fuck Jim..."

"Ah, it's not a big deal. Not hard for an electrician to find work, but that's not the point."

"What's the point?"

"There is no point. That's the fucking point," he says, snorting loudly. "Sometimes I wish I was back in Afghanistan... you know? Back where it was okay to be insane. I have these nightmares... and as horrifying as they are, filled with blood and explosions and pale dead faces lying cold upon the hot desert sand... I find myself waking up thinking that I'm back over there, and you know the craziest thing, I always end up feeling rotten when I realize I'm not..."

"Do you want me to... I don't know, take you to a hospital, or... something?"

He shakes his head, staring off out the window again.

"Well, will I see you at the meeting next week?"

"Yeah, should be," he sighs. "Unless I'm dead."

And this final statement hangs in the air like a cloud of mustard gas, sucking the oxygen from the room, and by the way he's looking out the window, his lips pulled back into a thin line, and his hands that quiver with every breath he takes, I can tell he's not joking, and the possibility of him dying is a very real and tangible reality in his own mind. Outside a bird chirps it's lonely song, and the sound of sirens float through the window somewhere a couple blocks away. I can hear a baby crying and combined with all of this, I decide it's time to leave before I collapse in the wake of the sheer bleakness of it all.

I watch Jim dab at his crouch, and as he makes the grim realization that he's pissed in his pants, I say an awkward good-bye and head for the door.

"Mark," he calls just before I make my exit. I turn around and wait for him to say something, but the room remains silent, and after thirty seconds I decide that whatever it was he wanted to say has either been lost or repressed, and so I leave. As I exit the building I feel an empty burning inside of me as a sinister voice whispers between my ears; did you enjoy that, Marky boy? That there's your future, so I hope you took it all in, the glory of being a middle-aged single alcoholic piece of shit. That's the life for you, brother. That's the life you've chose!

Fuck you alcohol, for turning us into savages. Fuck addiction and all of its devilish ways of tricking us. Fuck cigarettes and cocaine and everything else that offers the illusion of freedom and fun, but in reality only leads to death and destruction. Fuck you cancer, for infecting my body and trying to spread. For growing grotesque lumps on my testicle and making it so that I can't have another child... And on another note, fuck you terrorists for making me feel nervous when I go out to the Sens game and have to walk through metal detectors. Fuck you for causing me to unfairly judge anyone wearing a turban with a beard. Fuck you for making me racist. Fuck you for making it so that I am constantly envisioning horrific explosions and guns and blood while I pass by crowds in the street. Fuck you Media for betraying our trust and cultivating this idea that we should be scared. Fuck you for helping the Terrorists win by idolizing them and showering them with air time on your networks. Fuck you for leading with blood and horror and tragedy. And for your goddamn segments on Kim Kardashian. You have helped create a society full of media whores, attention starved narcissists looking for their one chance to make it big, to go viral, to have a goddamn hashtag named after them. Fuck you Kim Kardashian and your entire family. Fuck you Bruce Jenner, or Kaitlyn, or whatever the fuck you'd like to be called. I don't give a shit whether you have a dick or not, it's your choice, live with it. Don't subject me to your insecurities in your vain attempt to gain fame. You are no hero to me. Fuck you politically correct Nazis who want to condemn me and call me a homophobic-sadistic-misogynist who doesn't care about the environment just because I don't cry every time I see someone drinking from a paper cup. Fuck you for not allowing me to say Merry Christmas. And for pushing your liberal agenda on me to the point where you are exploiting those who you claim to be defending. Fuck you politicians for allowing this to happen. And while I'm at it, fuck you teachers, fuck you police, and fuck anyone in a position of power who thinks they know better than us. Fuck the politicians for lying to us about who shot JFK. And fuck you for allowing food corporations and medical corporations to use us as their own person lab rats, feeding us addictive medication and genetically modified food with absolutely no idea what the side effects will be. Fuck you for stealing our tax dollars for your first-class plane rides and $20 glasses of orange juice. Fuck you teachers for telling me I can do anything. Fuck you for telling me to go to university. Guess what, IT WAS A WASTE OF FUCKING MONEY! Fuck you for telling me I'd never have a calculator in my pocket later in life. Guess what? Got one right here your dumb bitches, it's called a cell phone, and I spent seven hundred fucking dollars on it. On that note, fuck you Apple, and Google, and all the rest of you monopolizing cunts who charge us too much for data while you manufacture your phones using child labour in Vietnam and Bangladesh. And fuck you for selling our information to the government. Fuck you cops for shooting black people. Fuck you for perpetuating stereotypes. Fuck you for turning these biases into realities through your endless persecution of the same people. Fuck you for spying on me and then lying about it. Fuck you bankers for stealing our money and laughing about it while you sit in your penthouse boardrooms snorting cocaine and thinking of more ways to rip off the general public. And fuck you for making me think I can actually afford to buy that house down in Rockdale. But most of all, Fuck me. Fuck me for allowing myself to be manipulated and brainwashed. Fuck my superficial lust and my constant hypocrisy. Fuck me for feeling sorry for myself and not working as hard as I can, for being bitter and pessimistic and for always expecting the worst in people. And finally, fuck me for thinking that you'd actually care.

There's another eviction notice taped to the front door which I absent-mindedly rip up and crumble between my trembling hands. Who the fuck cares? What do I need a house for? It's not as if I have a family anymore. What's the bloody point? I have failed. My procrastinations and half-assed self-reassurances that tomorrow will be better have culminated in the irreversible catastrophe of my attempted life...

And suddenly, this liberating feeling washes over me.

I am free.

I take another slug from the bottle of rye which I've been consuming at an aggressive rate during my drive home. The liquor makes me cough and cringe for a moment, and then I am moving again, down the hallway and into the living room of my empty house.

Fuck the chains of expectations and responsibilities. I can feel a rushing tingle setting in, between my flesh and bones, and without really acknowledging it, I begin to move through the house, my brain on a momentary vacation. NO VACANCY. My mind is closed. You may knock but no one will answer. Please leave your name and number at the beep.

I see my daughter waiting for me in the living room. Her pale lips are pulled back in a revolting sneer, and she points at me again with her goddamn skeleton finger. Blood leaks from her ears and nose, and there appears to be a rope tied around her waist. It takes me a moment to realize that it's actually her umbilical cord.

Burn it down, she whispers inside my head.

"Not a bad idea, sweetie," I say to the empty room, smiling. "Not a bad idea at all."

I pass through the kitchen, taking faint notice of Tracey's letter which is still sitting all stale on the round kitchen table like an old casserole. I burst into the garage full of purpose, and I can feel a fire in my loins as I scoop up the gasoline canister from the cement floor.

I've always loved the smell of gas, and the sweet scent fills my nostrils as I open the cap. I stand there in the doorway between the garage and the kitchen as my subconscious scrambles ferociously to force me to reconsider what I am contemplating... and I stand there all glassy eyed attempting to draw some sort of significance or sentimentality from my empty house, but as the simple truth dawns on me, I suppose it was already too late anyways, but this one truth hits me like a goddamn torpedo; a house is worthless without a family.

And then, I begin pouring.

I delight in the act of dumping copious amounts of gas all over Trace's fine china cabinet, seeing my own smirking face in the reflection of the porcelain plates. The man staring back at me is a stranger. A hollow-eyed beast with lips that curl upwards in a sinister smile.

"I told you one day I would destroy you!" I yell at the china cabinet.

Momentarily, I contemplate whether I've lost my mind...

But I drown that disturbing thought below the surface of my subconscious, taking another long swig from the Forty Creek bottle. La-la-la I'm not crazy la-la-la.

I cannot be deterred, I am committed! For perhaps the first time in my life, I am committing to something. A shame it turns out to be my complete and utter destruction.

I douse the living room; the television, the couch, the credenza against the wall with all those framed pictures of my wife and son, and looking at them now, they almost seem imaginary, mere figments of my deranged and twisted mind.

My feet are drenched and I can feel the gas all slimy and hot between my toes. For some unknown and perplexing reason, this makes me feel like dancing, and so I start prancing around the house like Tom Cruise in Risky Business, splashing gasoline all over my beautiful hardwood floors, slipping and sliding around like a child outside in the rain, and in my heart, I feel a swell as laughter bursts from my contorted lips, echoing throughout the empty house as my own insanity mocks me. I feel good.

The canister finally runs dry and I toss it aside into the corner of the living room. That sick sweet smell filling my nose and making me feel light headed. If only Trace could see...

I wonder what my son would think. This sort of behavior would certainly fall into the anti-establishment persona which he seems so intent on keeping up. I back myself up to the front door and take a deep breath, the stink of gasoline filling my nostrils. My daughter is standing by the staircase, her long black hair covering most of her face, and she nods approvingly at me, her head all bent sideways and neck twisting. She flashes her yellow teeth and says, "Do you need a light, daddy?"

"Got one right here baby," I say, opening the closet and reaching into the pocket of my winter jacket. I find a pack of matches from the cigar room at the Hilton Suites in Gatineau, which I had frequented over the winter with Dick. The pack is all bent and misshapen, but the matches on the inside appear to be intact, and so taking one last look around the house, the smell of gasoline thick like fog around me, I lighten the entire row of matches in one foul swoop, and with the front door open, I toss the burning wicks to the floor, and it's slightly disturbing the indifference with which I complete this action, but I cannot question the cosmos.

My body is being propelled by something greater, something I cannot control, and I give my dead daughter the thumbs up as I back out of the front door, watching the flames race down the hallways towards the stairs, the orange tips licking up the walls, and a sound that sort of resembles breathing. The fire is breathing. That was some poetic shit.

I am struck suddenly, as the black smoke begins to billow from my still open front door, that I have nowhere to go really, and although this fact should cause me much anxiety and panic, I cannot be bothered to stress over it, because really, what the fuck matters at this point?

Another shot of whiskey will help. Ah, yup, down the drain she goes. My mind is dancing upon the grave of my own life. I am the king of nothing. The lord of nowhere. The prince of ambivalence. Give me my crown you bastards, but don't be offended when I take a shit in it.

Sunday

My phone keeps buzzing upon my desk. It could be any number of people, I suppose, but most likely it's Trace calling to inquire as to the state of our residence. My head feels like its clogged with fiberglass, tiny stars dancing upon the black curtains of my closed eyelids.

I'm lying on the floor in my office, as I have been since late last night. I stopped by the Royal Oak on Bank and Lisgar (The Dirty Oak as it was so eloquently dubbed), and proceeded to drain three pitchers and about six shots of whiskey over the course of about four hours, at which point I was asked to kindly vacate the premises.

Bzzz-bzzz-bzzz.

"Shut-up," I say out loud to my phone.

Suddenly, I am jolted by a loud banging coming from the front door.

Thump-thump-thump.

Is that someone at the door or is my heart finally having a conniption?

THUMP-THUMP-THUMP!

Okay, no, that's someone at the office door.

I rise sluggishly from the carpeted floor and make my way to the front entrance. The right side of my face is swollen and puffy, and I can feel the colour red rushing from it. The goose egg from where Cheryl hit me with the glass appears to have gone down, which is good, I guess.

I snap to attention when I notice the police cruiser parked out front through the glass walls of the office. The cop is peering in through them, using his hand to shield the glare. I nod at him and quickly move for the office door. I can tell through the glass that he is a large man, broad shoulders, a mustache and chubby cheeks. He has a substantial gut that seems to be forgiven by the size of his arms and chest.

"Mr. Stanfield?" he says.

"Yes," I say, stepping outside and letting the door close behind me. "What can I do for you, officer?"

"Are you aware your house burned down last night?"

"Pardon?"

"Your house. It was set on fire last night. Evidence suggests arson."

"Oh...my."

"Oh my indeed. Where were you last night, Mr. Stanfield?"

"Last night?"

"Yes, at approximately 5:30pm?"

"Well... I was... here. Working away. You know, gotta keep that gravy train rolling..."

"I understand that your house was very close to being foreclosed on, is that correct Mr. Stanfield?"

"Well, ya know, the bank mentioned something along those lines. I was planning on paying them though, truly I was."

"What do you mean by planning?"

"I mean I intended to pay them, you know, but the thing is, you need money to pay people, right? So, I was here, working. Working damn hard, trying to sell a home so I could keep mine."

"And did you manage to sell a home, Mr. Stanfield?"

"Oh god no."

"Mr. Stanfield," the cop says, sighing in a way that someone who deals with liars everyday of their lives is apt to do when they know someone is lying to them, "you look... shabby. Where did you sleep last night?"

"Well, here... on the floor."

"Why?"

"My wife... she left and... you know, I've been sort of, I don't know, sad about it."

"Sad?"

"Yes."

"You reek of alcohol, Mr. Stanfield."

"It's my new cologne," I say foolishly.

"This is no time for jokes, Mr. Stanfield."

"Oh, I hear you officer, I do. I mean, everything has gotten so serious lately. Did I mention that my wife just had a miscarriage?"

"Oh... well..." the cop stalls, some of the macho gusto evaporating from his eyes.

"Yup, dead. The baby died inside of her. It was a daughter, you see, and I was so scared to have a daughter, no kidding, I thought it would be just about the worst thing that could happen. The worst. I mean, how the fuck am I supposed to raise a little girl in a society where kids are sending dick pics before the age of thirteen? Honestly? Can you tell me?"

"I... don't have a daughter, so..."

"But you know what? I was wrong. I was so wrong. Because I know what the worst thing is now, I truly do. I feel it in my stomach, rotten to the core like a bad peach. I really am a vile and disgusting individual, because I know, deep down, part of me was hoping the baby would die. How fucked up is that, eh? But you can't deny your subconscious, you know?"

"I guess not," the cop says, lips pulled back in a grim frown. "Sir..."

"And now she's following me around, everywhere I go, she's pointing at me and foaming at the mouth and she wants me to fuck her... I think."

At this point I can see I have effectively creeped this policeman out to the point where he's actually taking steps away from me, shuffling backwards and continuing to frown.

"Did I mention I have cancer? In my balls. Yup, in my fucking balls. I got something growing down there, some sort of tumor."

"Okay, Mr. Stanfield... I'm going to... leave now. But... we may need to contact you again for further statement."

"Oh by all means, call me anytime good-sir. Stop by and we can share a glass of rum. I'd really appreciate the company, to be honest."

The cop shakes his head in bewilderment and rushes to his car, speeding off without giving me a second glance.

Please enter the four-digit passcode for Voicemail:

Beep.

Markus! What in the fucking Christ did you do? Our house, our clothes, everything, the goddamn pictures... my computer, my writing. I had dozens of stories in my office. You fucking bastard. You fucking selfish prick piece of lying shit...

Beep.

...goddamn disgraceful pig. Do you have no remorse at all? How could you do this to us? The insurance guys are saying we'll be lucky to get a goddamn cent on account of the arson, and it certainly doesn't help that you are the number one fucking suspect. The police have called me three fucking times Markus... THREE FUC-

Beep.

-CKING TIMES! What are we going to do? You have to fix this. Call me back you coward. I expect to hear from you before days' end. Thomas is livid. He had his whole life in that house. His winter clothes, his drawings from when he was a child... and your father is worried sick. He's out driving around the streets with Ping looking for you."

Beep.

Goddamn your fucking voicemail, and goddamn you Markus, goddamn you all the way to hell. Fucker.

Beep.

Hello, this message is for Markus Stanfield. This is Shirley Thompson from Toronto Dominion Bank of Canada, and we are calling to inquire as to the status of payment on your outstanding mortgage. As indicated in our recent correspondence, you have less than thirty days to make full payment on your balance owing, or an eviction notice will be served and we will be forced to foreclose on your house. I trust this message will...

Beep.

Hello, Mr. Stanfield, this is Brian Norris from All State Insurance. We are contacting you in regards to your recent claim, submitted by your wife, Mrs. Tracey Stanfield. We have some questions we need to ask and would appreciate if you could call us back at your earliest convenience."

Beep.

Did your wife like the pictures I sent her? I have more if she wants them. I expect she always knew how small your cock was, but those pictures really capture it's sheer miniscule size, don't you think? You fat old fuck. Did you really think you could just leave me? You wanted the last laugh, eh? The last word. Well fuck you Mark, and your small dick. I hope you rot in hell.

Beep.

Dad, what the fuck? Mom is freaking out. Did you actually burn our house down? I'm worried about you, as much as you don't deserve that. Where are you, seriously? You need to call mom. I'm on my way back from Kingston. I don't even care about all my stuff... I'm scared. Our family is... it's fucked, dad. Seriously, call mom.

Beep.

Voicemail is Full.

I pass out again in the back office with my face plastered against the carpet and my hand on my cancerous testicle. I tried jerking off but whether imaginary or real, I kept feeling this pain in my nut so, I couldn't nut. Fucking cancer. What an asshole.

My dreams swell inside my demented mind. Flashes of flames climbing up the walls. A dead foetus covered in blood. Running, down a hallway. Or a field. And there's something chasing me, although I'm not quite sure what it is. A man in a mask with a horrid grin. There's a wall, with men chained to it, their limbs rotting, covered in insects, lips all caked with blood. I try to release them but they tell me to leave them alone. They don't need my help. They laugh at me; ridiculing me, pointing with their withered fingers. He doesn't see, they whisper to one another. He cannot see the chains on his own arms. And they continue to snicker at me as I back away, moving from the shadows into the light... the bright shining light, staring directly into it... Markus! Markus!

"Markus!"

I awake to find my father standing over me, his hands around my shoulders as he shakes me gently upon the floor of my office.

"What in God's name are you doing here?" he asks, his face pulled back in concern as his bushy white eyebrows twitch.

"Sleeping, obviously."

"What happened to your head?"

"Oh, this..." I say, reaching up and feeling the bump from where Cheryl struck me with the glass. "It's nothing, just a scratch."

"Don't be a jackass," he says, "come on, let's get you up off the floor."

He scoops me up from under my armpits and hoists me upright. My legs are tingling as the blood rushes back into them, and I can feel a small knot in my lower back that will undoubtedly cause me much distress in the coming days. I cough and rub at my eyes while my father continues to look upon me as if I've just been resurrected or something.

"What are you doing here?" I ask him.

"I asked you the same damn thing," he says, crossing his arms stubbornly.

"I told you, I was sleeping."

"Is that because you burned your house down last night?"

"No," I shake my head. "It's because I've been working day and night to try and close a deal."

"Oh, so you expect me to believe that you were working late, and in your diligence and determination, you simply passed out on the floor of your office?"

"Sure," I shrug. "The cops seemed to find it reasonable enough."

"Oh, you think so, eh?"

I shrug again.

"Well, they've called me twice already. Lots of questions. About you. About Trace. About everything. Why didn't you come to me if you were having money troubles? You know I have a nice nest saved up, I could have helped you, I could have..."

"I don't want your help," I say, staring at the carpet.

"Well that's too damn bad," my father says, grabbing me by the

172

elbow like the cop should have done earlier. "I'm taking you out of here."

"But... I've got nowhere to go."

"Don't be stupid," he says, looking at me with a grimace. "You've got a place to go whether you want to accept it or not. And frankly, I don't give a damn at this point. You're coming to my place, and Ping is going to cook us dinner, and you're going to fucking sit there and tell me what in the Christ is going on because at this point, I'm not sure whether you're even my son anymore. I hardly recognize you, Mark. You look bloody awful."

"Oh that's rich," I say, pulling my arm from his grasp. "Now all of a sudden you give a damn. It didn't stop you from running off with some Filipino whore the minute mom dropped dead, running around town with her hanging off your arm, without so much as a visit to mom's tombstone..."

His fist strikes me in the eye with surprising force, and I stumble backwards, reeling and reaching, I whirl to the side and fall against the wall. I can feel my eye swelling already, and I prod at it gently with my fingertips. "Good shot, old man," I say, chuckling.

"Your mother would be ashamed of you right now, Mark," he says. "And I think you know that. But I'm done with your guilt. I'm done trying to apologize for something that needs no apology. I'm your goddamned father, and I'm the only one you've got left who can help you. Whether you want to admit that or not is up to, but I'm done putting up with your bullshit. Now get in the fucking car."

And with that, my old man walks out the front door, letting it slam behind him, and I am left standing against the wall with my swollen eye. Goddamnit. Earl Stanfield, you never cease to amaze.

"Fuck it," I sigh, and follow him out the door.

We drive in silence along the country roads outside of Armprior, the sun setting in front of us, its bottom half disappearing along the horizon. I lean my head against the window and close my eyes. There's a dull throb beating softly against the raised flesh of my right eye from where Earl cold clocked me. The old man could still pack a punch; I had to give him that.

I feel the car come to a stop and open my eyes.

"You coming?" Earl asks from outside, peering down through the open driver's side door.

"Yeah, yeah," I say, my eye aching at each and every movement. I exit the car and make for the front door, walking up the brick pathway (which was constructed by landscapers whom I had recommended).

A blue light descends over the sky as the sun fully disappears under the treeline, and I look over at my father, my one eye all swollen and squinting, but he's not looking at me, and I can tell the old man is pretty pissed off.

Suddenly, the front door is flung open and I hear; "Oh herro!"

There it is. Now I remember why I hate him!

"Hi sweetie," Earl says, giving her a kiss on the cheek as he strides in past her.

"Oh hi Mawk!" Ping says, a big stupid smile plastered upon her face. "Wha' happen to yo' I?"

"Hi Ping," I say with a sigh. "Oh this, I ran into a door."

"You must be mo' carefur!"

"You're probably right, Ping. You're probably right."

Inside, the house smells of foreign spices, and I can't deny it smells pretty damn good. I reflect on the fact that I haven't eaten in over twenty-four hours, and my stomach does a summersault to emphasize this point.

"You hug-wee, Mawk?"

"Yeah, I could eat."

I catch my father, who is in the process of hanging his jacket, shoot me a look, and so I quickly add, "thank-you please!"

"Oh! You wer-come!"

I follow her into the kitchen and am struck with a heavy dose of déjà vu. I can picture my mother standing exactly where Ping is standing, her arms crossed, shaking her head at me. She looks disappointed in me, and I guess that makes sense, given that my entire life is one giant goddamn disappointment. I sit down at the kitchen table and lean my aching head in my withered palms. The bright light in the kitchen causes me to squint.

Ping scoops some noodles and veggies into a bowl for me and tops it off with some chicken. The steam rising from the food hits my nostrils and sends me into a frenzy. I start shovelling the noodles into my mouth, barely taking breaks to breathe, and I devour the entire bowl within a couple of minutes.

"Wow, you hug-wee!" Ping exclaims. "You wrike?"

"Yes, I wrike," I tell her. She smiles and nods while my father enters the room, shaking his head at my use of the accent.

"At least show a bit of damn respect when you're in my house, eh?" he says gruffly, scooping himself some dinner into a bowl.

I wash my bowl and place it in the dishrack. My father finishes his meal, gives me a weird look, and declares that he is going to bed. I give faint notice that it's only 8:30 and I almost call out to him, but I can tell the old man has some reflecting to do, and so I leave it. Ping is sitting across from me staring blankly at my forehead, and since this sort of creeps me out, I get up and wander into the living room.

There's a wraparound leather couch, all white, which goes well with the egg-shell coloured walls. A mantle filled with framed pictures sits over a space where there could be a fireplace, but ol' Earl never bothered to get one installed.

I don't feel much like watching TV, and so I scoop up one of ma's old Tom Clancy novels that are stashed beneath the coffee table, and begin flipping through the pages.

I make it about two pages before getting bored (thank you internet for obliterating my attention span). I discard the novel and rise from the couch, making my way across the wide living room over towards the mantle, where a dozen or more framed photographs wait to greet me. The pictures were just as my mother had left them, that much I could tell. My father either didn't have the heart to move them, or like most men, failed to really notice them at all. My money was on the latter.

Of course, the first thing I see is a goddamnit family portrait of Trace, Thomas and I, standing in front of our brand new house like the proud young adults that we thought we were. Oh, you poor bastard. Look at you; standing all tall and proud with that naïve smile spread across your face, oh so oblivious. Even Thomas looks happy in the picture, which strikes a chord inside my chest.

"Yo' howse gon?"

"Jesus!" I say, jumping and whirling around to find Ping standing behind me. "Yes," I nod after composing myself. "My house gone."

"Ah," Ping says seriously, staring a moment at the photograph in my hands, then shifting her eyes back into my own. "No rove?"

"No," I sigh. "I suppose there wasn't."

We stand there in silence for a few moments, and she reaches out suddenly and pulls me in with incredible force, wrapping her arms around me and squeezing. "Rove here," she says, looking up at me...

At this point, I guess I sort of break down and, really, I can't remember all that well, but I sort of start sobbing and Ping takes me over to the couch and sits beside me while my father comes out of his bedroom down the hall, looking all red-faced and stormy, but when he sees me and Ping sitting there on the couch, her one arm still wrapped around my shoulder, I see the anger fade from his face like a stone sinking in a lake, and he comes over and gives me a hug from the other side and says, "It's good to see you again, son."

After a while, I manage to regain my composure, and I look up into my father's eyes and say solemnly, "Dad, can we have a goddamn drink, please?"

The three of us are sitting around the kitchen table, my father and I with glasses of scotch clutched firmly between our hands. "It's made of oak," my dad says.

"Yeah, I know. You've told me about a thousand times already."

"Oh," he laughs, taking a sip form his short tumbler glass half full of scotch. "I suppose I have."

"That's okay," I say. "It's a good table." The scotch has effectively numbed my swollen and bruised eye at this point, which is comforting.

"Ay, that it is."

"I miss mom."

"I miss her too, Mark."

"Do you really, though?" I ask him, taking another pull from my own scotch glass. I take faint notice of my wobbling hand and wonder how drunk I am. We had been sitting around the table for at least an hour now, and this was either my fourth or fifth glass of scotch.

"What do you mean?" my father asks, leaning forward against the table.

"Well," I say, gesturing with my eyes towards Ping and then shrugging my shoulders (yeah, real subtle you jackass).

Earl sighs at this point, setting his drink down and staring across the table at me with concrete eyes. "You've never understood. Maybe you never will. Maybe you don't want to. Either way, doesn't change a damn thing. It doesn't change the fact that I miss your mother more than words can describe. I dream of her most every night, did you know that? And I wake up every morning thinking she's still here... sometimes, I swear Mark, I can smell her in the bed beside me. But she's gone. She's..." he sighs again, taking a hit of the scotch. He grimaces and coughs the cough of a man whom has just swallowed too much scotch in one gulp. After a moment, he continues. "Can't you see that Ping helped me? She saved my life, really. She was what got me through the grief, the sorrow filled days when I didn't want to get out of bed. I don't know why it happened this why. I don't know how... and I don't want to know. All you need to know it that I love her, and always will. But that doesn't mean I've forgotten about your mother... it doesn't mean that..."

My father wipes his eyes and slugs back the rest of his scotch. He smacks his lips and smiles, turning his eyes back to me. "You wanna see something?"

He stands with a grin on his face, taking Ping's hand and waving with his other for me to follow. He leads us through the living room and down the hallway which runs deeper into the house. We pass by the master bedroom and turn into the last door on the left.

"Wasn't this your office?"

"Yeah," my dad replies gruffly. "What the hell did I need an office for anyways?" he laughs. "Never did a minute of bloody work in here. I think it's just something people like to say... they have a home office... or whatever."

I can tell that my father is now drunk, which is refreshing to me in a way that I cannot describe.

Earl flicks on the light and I am greeted with dozens of paintings strung about the room.

"Ping made these," Earl says, sweeping his arm across the room.

There are several pictures of Ping and my father. These weren't Da Vinci's or anything, but they did have a certain loveliness to them.

"Mom used to like to paint..."

"Yes," my father says. "She did."

And that's when I notice the painting in the easel. It's the whole Stanfield clan sitting around my dining room table at Easter; Trace and I, my son and Alycia (or Alyssa or Aiysha), Earl and Ping, and even my monster of a mother-in-law, all of us turned towards the invisible camera and smiling these amazing smiles, looking truly happy in the midst of a fabulous turkey dinner. It was a picture right out of a Scott Fitzgerald novel.

"Famiry," Ping says, pointing at the painting.

"Yes, family," I say, patting my father on the back. I can see that he is drunkenly crying again, the old bastard. Never could handle his booze.

Monday

The next morning, I awake on my father's living room couch with a slight throbbing in my head, and I yelp in pain as I bring my hand up to my face to press on it, momentarily forgetting about how my father slugged me in the eye the evening previous. I can tell the eye is still swollen, and undoubtedly had developed some colour over the course of the night. I feel that the gash from where Cheryl struck me with the glass has begun to scab over, which is good, I guess?

I felt good, though.

The morning is a cloudy one, mere freckles of sunlight making it through the window, dancing upon the hardwood floor. Still, the bastard was trying to break through. Who knows? It could turn out to be a nice day.

I smell coffee and make my way into the kitchen.

"Morning!" Ping says, pouring me a cup.

"Morning, Ping."

My father sits with the newspaper open at the kitchen table, which makes me feel suddenly fifteen years old again.

"So, Mark," he says, not bothering to lower the paper from in front of his face. "What exactly are we going to do about your situation?"

"To be frank," I say pulling out a chair across from him. "I'm not even sure where to start."

"Well, you should probably call Tracy. I'd say that's step one."

"Yeah, that might be an idea..."

He looks at me from over the paper at this point, and I let out a sigh as I rise from my chair.

I walk into the living room and scoop up my phone from the

coffee table. I cringe to see a barrage of text messages from Cheryl. Most of them reading like a high school girl's diary. I'M GOING TO KILL MYSELF! FUCK YOU OLD MAN! ANSWER ME!!!

Suddenly, my phone rings in my hands, causing me to jump. The number shows up Unknown, which makes me hesitate. From the entranceway of the kitchen I can see my father's head leaning into view, and he gives me a look that says pick up that goddamn phone, son. And so I do.

"Hello?"

"Is this Markus Stanfield?" an unfamiliar male voice inquires.

"Yes, well, maybe. Who's asking?"

"This is Spence Price, Member of Parliament for Ottawa – Orleans. And I'm calling you today to discuss my wife."

And I let the fact that he introduces himself formally slide, despite how absurd it is under the circumstances. "Cheryl?" I say stupidly, instantly covering my mouth with my hand. But it's too late. Her name has been spoken (by a very unprepared and stupid man).

"Yes... she, well, she's in the hospital."

I am speechless, and my mouth hangs dumbly as I breathe heavily into the phone.

"She tried to commit suicide last night," Spencer Price, Member of Parliament for Ottawa – Orleans continues. "I think we should meet."

"Meet?"

"Yes, there's some details that we need to discuss, I think."

"Okay," I sigh. "I'm sorry to hear... I mean... I don't really know what to say..."

"Thank you for your concern, it is much appreciated."

"Okay..."

"I would like to meet with you," he says. "I have something for you."

What in Christ's name could he have for me?

"Are you available today?"

"Umm, I'll have to check..."

"It really is very important."

"Okay, where do you want to meet?" I say, hoping I suppressed the melodramatic sigh enough for him not to notice.

"How about the Second Cup on Kent Street, it's close to my office."

"Sure, fine. What time?"

"Can you make it in an hour?"

I look into the kitchen where my father is studying me with raised eyebrows. "Yes," I sigh. "I will see you in an hour."

I hang up and feel a numbness setting in, somewhere in the pit of my stomach. My eye throbs and I wonder if this is all some sort of sick joke. Some sort of elaborate ploy or prank that is meant to see my fragile state of mind finally shattered. At this point, the idea is not unappealing to me. Shit, at least if I was insane I wouldn't understand just how completely and irrevocably fucked I am. My father shakes his head knowingly as I inform him that I have to run out to take care of an errand.

"I'll be back by this afternoon," I assure him.

"Try not to burn anything down."

"No promises," I say, although in my head I am more concerned about being blamed for the attempted suicide of my mistress by her husband, who just so happens to be a Federal Representative for the Canadian Government. Poor life choice, Markus, really, really, loose decisions.

I make it to the front door and realize that my car is still at the office. "Hey dad," I call out, "can I borrow your car?"

Jesus, I really was a goddamn teenager again. But one quick look down at my gut confirms that I am in fact still an overweight middle-aged man who needs to borrow his daddy's car.

Life, you are one cruel bitch, you know that?

I'm sitting at a table for two in Second Cup clutching a cup of black coffee, my fingers playing a constant drumroll upon the cardboard cup, tap-tap-tap. I took a spot by the back which faces the door, and I survey every person who enters the coffee shop like I'm fucking James Bond, waiting for the inevitable.

I can't help but notice the barrage of odd stares I receive from the patrons as they study my battered face. I suppose I did look a bit out of place, what with the black eye and scab on my forehead, but hey, at least they are finally noticing me!

Jesus Cheryl, why did you have to put me in this situation?

She must have known.

She must have planned for it to happen this way, that calculating bitch. And yes, I am disturbed with the complete lack of empathy and sorrow I am displaying right now, in case you are wondering. But in all honesty, I've had quite a week, on top of one helluva mediocre life, and so if I'm being one hundred percent genuine here, I don't have any sympathy for Cheryl, or anyone else for that matter, who has tried to kill themselves, because if I haven't fucking done it yet, then what in Christ's name is your excuse, huh?

The bell over the door rings, and I see Spencer Price stroll into the shop, hands in the pockets of his Armani blue-pin striped three-piece suit, his jet-black hair gelled perfectly to the side.

"Markus," he says, approaching the table. "Do you mind if I get a coffee first?"

"Go for it... man," I say, dumbfounded.

"Thank you," he responds.

I watch the robot go over to the barista and he obviously saying something dry and witty because she giggles and gives him a bat of her eye lashes, and I can't help but wonder if I've somehow slipped into an alter reality... what in the fuck is going on here?

Finally, the Honourable Spencer Price finally sits down across from me, taking a sip from his coffee and simply sitting there for a moment, staring across at me with unwavering eyes.

I watch him study my black eye briefly, and a flash of recognition moves behind his eyes. This man has been struck in the face recently.

Then, he moves to pull something from his suit jacket.

This is it, I think to myself. The pistol is coming out. He's going to whack me right here in the Second Cup. Fuck it, I probably deserve it anyways; if not for Cheryl, then a dozen other indictable offenses over the course of my misspent life.

But then he pulls out a sealed envelope, setting it on the table and sliding it over towards me.

"What is that?" I ask him.

"It's a letter," he says.

"What sort of letter?" I say, fearing a subpoena or some other form of pending litigation.

"It's from Cheryl," he sighs. "She left this on the bed... it's, well, it's addressed to you."

Jesus Christ.

I scoop the letter up off the table and see my name scrolled sloppily upon the front in misshapen letters.

"So, how did she... you know..."

"She swallowed an entire bottle of Xanax."

"Ah... I see."

"Yes, it was truly an unfortunately incident."

"An unfortunate incident?"

"Yes, very much so."

"And she's going to be okay?" I ask.

"Yes," he says, sipping his coffee. "She's in General right now, in the ICU. But the doctors were able to successfully purge the pills from her body before they could do too much damage."

"Well, that's.... good?"

"How long have you known my wife?" he asks, clasping his hands together in front of his mouth and leaning his elbows on the table.

"Oh, not too long, you know, a year... or two, maybe..."

"And you two were lovers?"

"Uh, yeah, I suppose we were."

He nods knowingly, "Well, I trust we can keep this mess between us, like responsible adults. No one needs to hear about the complexities of this situation, that is my opinion."

I actually start laughing at this point, much to his chagrin.

"What, Mr. Stanfield, may I ask is so funny?"

"You've got to be fucking kidding me," I say, chuckling. "Here you are, sitting across from the man who is fucking you wife, and you're more concerned about your own damn reputation. Oh, we fucked hard, in case you were wondering. Some of the best sex I've ever had, if I'm being completely honest..."

"You watch your fucking mouth you piece of shit..." he snarls, spit foaming suddenly at the corners of his lips. His eyes were black marbles and it was actually refreshing to confirm that this man was in fact human, and not some robotic replica of what a human is supposed to be. "I know who you are. You think I don't have access to certain information, Mr. Stanfield? You're a pathetic drunk of a real estate agent who hasn't sold a home in over a year. You're behind on just about every bill you have, and from what I can see, you're about one month away from insolvency..."

"You got it, bucko. Which is unfortunate for you, isn't it? Since there's literally nothing you can do to threaten me..."

He stares at me in disbelief from across the table, while I mouth the words fuck you to him with a twisted grin plastered upon my face.

"Well," he says, rising from his seat and buttoning up his suit jacket with the well-practiced hands of a man who wears a suit every goddamn day of his life. "I think we're done here, Mr. Stanfield."

"Oh, we're done," I tell him, looking at him with shaking eyes. "You can rest easy, by the way. I'm not going to call the goddamn Citizen or anything. That's for Cheryl, just so you know."

"That's fine," he nods, extending his bulbous hand across the table, "and I sincerely hope we can count on your support in 2019."

Spencer Price's hand hangs in the air for a few more moments like a feather caught in the wind, until finally he pulls it back and turns to leave.

He turns around to say something, but after being met with the many wandering eyes in the coffee shop, he thinks better of it and leaves.

Dear Markus,

I'm sorry for how it all ended. I never wanted things to end up that way. In truth, I don't think I've known just exactly what I've wanted for some time now... that's what being caught up in a bad marriage can do. I guess I've always been weak. Ever since I was a little girl, I was always so dependent on those around me...

Does that make it my fault?

I don't know, but I know one thing; I can't go on feeling this way. I know I hide it well... I'm supposed be a strong independent woman... but I am lonely. So lonely, Mark... and I guess that makes me feel even worse, since I've always prided myself on being a strong woman, you know?

But I wanted you to know before I go, that it's not because of you.

Well, I mean, it's kind of because of you.

(I still can't believe you dumped me!)

But I'm not writing this to blame you.

I'm writing this to say thank-you.

Thank-you for opening my eyes to the fact that there is no solace in love.

I'm just tired of being unappreciated, I guess.

Does that make me selfish?

They say your spouse rubs off on you, so it would certainly make sense if I had become selfish... although, I suppose you've been rubbing off on me more than Spencer has lately!

Anyways, I'm getting tired now. The pills are kicking in. I can feel my eyes trying to roll back into my head. My tongue tastes funny. It feels puffy. Ha-ha-ha-ha, oh my, this is actually sort of fun. Who would have thought dying came with so many colours.

Good-bye, Markus. I know you don't love me, but I hope, maybe someday, you can think of me and have nice thoughts.

PS. Sorry for sending those pictures to your wife. I was drunk and desperate and... oh, I don't know, I'm a bitch, what can I say? I do really feel bad about that, though. Just so you know.

XOXOXO

Cheryl P.

"Why are you so angry, son?"

"Oh, I don't know," I say, pondering my father's question as we sit around the kitchen table. It's close to 8pm and I've been home for a few hours now. Ping has been scarce, giving my father and I the space we need. I filled him in on everything; Cheryl, the suicide letter, the pompous husband... it was nice to have somebody to talk to, to be honest. I told him about my mortgage, about the Scholaces, about the fact that I've been seeing the ghost of my dead daughter following me around. And the cancer. It all just came pouring out, like a broken faucet; once I got started I couldn't stop.

"Have I ever told you why I quit politics, dad?"

"You've mentioned little things here and there," he says. "Disingenuous cocksuckers I believe was a common phrase used."

"Well, they are, but it's not just that..." I sigh. "I can remember, back in 1999, when I was working for Larry Trample, you remember him?"

"I think so," my father nods, "you introduced us at some Christmas event at the Westin."

"Yeah, well, Larry showed me a lot. And it wasn't the fact that he left his wife for a twenty-five-year-old staffer, I mean, that was almost expected, you know? And it wasn't the fact that he made faulty expense claims or the fact that he seemed to actually believe that abortion was wrong... I mean it was all of those things combined, but there was this one time, when talks of invading the middle-east had started. People like to pretend those talks only came after 9-11, but that's not true. We were talking about it all throughout the 90s, really, and I remember this one time, I asked Larry what he thought about invading a country like Afghanistan, and you wanna know what he said?

"Markus, I don't know why we even bother. It's not like those savages will ever learn. We take one group of savages out of power and put another group of savages in their place. It's never going to change, and I don't think a single person in Simcoe gives a shit about what happens to Afghanistan. I think it's a waste of time and money, simple as that."

"And you want to know what killed me the most about that, dad?" I pause, taking a sip from my beer. "It's the fact that he wasn't wrong. I mean, look at how things are today. That fat bastard wasn't wrong, and I think I even knew as much back then, but I

186

just couldn't accept it. I couldn't accept that one of our elected representatives, a man who was supposed to be the pinnacle of our human nature, someone who was supposed to care about humanity, and the right to freedom of expression, freedom of religion, fuck, the right not to be bombed or tortured in your own home by your own fucking government, you know? But it was all a lie. Half of these MPs couldn't give you the definition of equality, and the other half use the word 'irregardless' in everyday conversations. It's all a lie, dad. I guess that's maybe why I've been so angry... but I mean, there's plenty of other reasons too, you know?"

My dad smiles, his eyes glowing in the dim light of the overhead lamp. "You remind me of your mother," he says.

"Mom was a much better person than me," I say, looking down at my beer glass.

"Don't cut yourself short, Mark. You've always been a sensitive boy," he says, "I used to be worried you were gay, you know?"

I look at my father in disbelief, shaking my head and chuckling to myself. Life, you truly are a cruel bitch.

My old man reaches out to me then, placing his hand on my arm. "We're with you, Mark. Whatever happens."

"Thanks," I say. "Fucking cancer."

"Hm mm," he responds. "Fucking cancer, indeed."

"Hey, at least I can get me some good medical grade dope to help with the Chemo."

"That shit makes me paranoid. It's too strong these days."

"Well shit, it's not as if I've got anything left to be paranoid about. My wife has left me, my mistress tried to kill herself, my son hates me, my dog is dead, I've got a black-eye because my dad socked me in the face, and my goddamn house was burned to the ground by a lunatic."

"Cheers!"

The sound of our beer bottles clinking together echoes in my ears as I take a long gulp from the bottle. And I can't help but think, despite the circumstances, what a nice and enjoyable evening this has been, which in turn causes me to wonder just exactly how much of my life I've wasted being miserable.

Tuesday

Tuesday morning arrives with a call from the Ottawa Police, who demand that I come downtown to the station to answer some questions.

"You should probably go face the music," my dad says.

"Yeah, yeah," I say. "I've seen enough A&E specials to know how to conduct myself in an interrogation room."

"Admit nothing," my dad nods.

I take my dad's car downtown and head into the station on Elgin, parking at the back of the lot beside a few ghost cars. I stroll through the lot with my head held high, doing my damnedest to look like a confident, innocent man. The hulking building casts an intimidating shadow, and the all-white walls seem far too clean for a white wall to be during this time of the year, but I suppose police were diligent if nothing else. I pass by empty cruisers in the parking lot, and an off-duty cop who is hacking a dart while he leans against his cruiser. He stares at me and gives me the internationally recognized man-to-man head nod as I pass.

I get to the front door and have to wait for someone to buzz me in. I walk past an officer encased behind a glass frame, who stares at me as I make my way through the front chamber. I am greeted by a burly cop at the other door, and he opens it for me, gesturing with a giant hand for me to enter.

It's the same cop who came to my office, and he studies me as I walk towards him with much concentration. He still can't tell whether I'm a lunatic or not, this much is clear by the way he lets me walk in front of him, keeping a few paces behind me the whole way down the long empty hallway.

"In here, Mr. Stanfield," he says from behind me. I turn around and he's got a door propped open leading into a mostly empty room save for a metal table with two chairs on either side. I take a seat at the far side and lean my elbows up against the surface of the imposing table. The walls are a bright white and an overhead light hangs above the table.

"So, Mr. Stanfield..."

"So... I'm sorry, I don't know your name."

"You can call me Sir," he replies gruffly. "Or Officer."

I start to chuckle but soon realize that he is in fact serious. I stare in bewilderment as Mr. Officer Sir shuffles through some loose pages, squinting his eyes and making slight head movements this way and that, doing his best to appear focused and competent. I can almost see the words I'm a serious man meant to be taken seriously carved into his pudgy face.

"So," he begins, setting the pages face down upon the table (I can only assume the contents of which contain doodles of cocks and balls and maybe a dinosaur). "You claim to be at your office for the duration of Saturday evening, the night in question?"

"Yeah, well, mostly..."

"What do you mean mostly?"

"Well, I may have stepped out for a drink at some point. It's highly likely, in fact."

"You like to have the odd drink, don't you Mr. Stanfield?"

"Who doesn't?"

"Oh plenty of us do not indulge in such vices, me included."

"Well," I sigh. "Drinking's not for the faint of heart."

"I assure you, Mr. Stanfield, I am not faint of heart."

"Want to have a drink then?"

"Enough," he says, slamming his fist on the table. "This is a serious issue and you are not taking things very seriously, Mr. Stanfield. Your attitude towards this whole situation is very suspect. Are you not upset over the fact that your house, along with all of your possessions, are gone?"

"Meh," I shrug. "I've never been a very materialistic man. I'm more concerned with the fact that my wife has left me, my son hates me, and I've got cancer in my balls. Oh did I mention my daughter..."

"I don't give a damn about your daughter, Mr. Stanfield. Or your balls for that matter. I want to know where you were Saturday night!"

"I told you, I was at the office, then the bar, then the office again, probably took a shit somewhere in there..."

"At exactly what time were you at the office?"

"Oh around 5 or 6."

"And when did you go to the bar?"

"Oh must have been around 6 or 7."

"And when did you leave the bar?"

"I was there rather late, I believe, right up until the bartender kicked me out."

"Hmm," Mr. Officer Sir nods, writing something down in his notepad.

"There's been reports of a young girl sighted in the area around the time the incident took place, can you speak on that?"

"A young girl?" I ask, dumbfounded.

"Yes, pale, long dark hair, wearing shabby looking clothing..."

"I... I don't know what to tell you."

"Were you involved with anyone that fits this description?" the son-of-a-bitch cop asks me with raised eye lids.

"No, thank you very much. I was not involved with any young girls."

"Hmmm," he swallows, jotting more notes.

We sit in silence for a while as Mr. Officer Sir writes in his notepad, stopping now and again to flip through the pages and study the words he has written. He scratches his head, bites his lip, and then looks back up at me.

"The truth is, Mr. Stanfield, we cannot prove that you burned down your house. I know you weren't at your office, but I have had reports that you were sitting at the Royal Oak on Bank Street until closing time, and lucky for you, this alibi does pretty much cover you, along with your corroborating report of events... although as to your whereabouts before the bar... you say you were at your office?"

"That's right, officer."

"Do you have any way of proving this? Security cameras? An email you sent from your computer?"

"Unfortunately, I don't have the budget for security cameras," I say. "And I was mostly looking over paperwork, you know? Studying the trends and such... looking for value in land that currently has none... just doing my job."

"Are you aware that Arson carries a potential sentence of fourteen years, Mr. Stanfield?"

"I was not aware."

"And intentionally lying during an interview, well that is considered Obstruction of Justice, Mr. Stanfield, which would carry additional sentencing and likely a large fine."

"Sounds serious."

"That will be enough, for now," he says. "I will have to ask you not to leave town without consulting us. We will likely have some follow-up questions for you."

I nod and get the hell out of there as fast as possible.

My phone vibrates in the cup holder beside me as I'm driving down the 417, cars sweeping by me like irrelevant blobs of light, like so many stars hurtling through the black, each star its own universe, and each universe completely oblivious to the existence of the next.

I pluck my phone out of the cup holder and study the caller ID.

Dr Von Hymen (yes, I am that crude, thank you very much).

I let the call go to voicemail, blanketing the very thought of dealing with my pending cancer treatment in a quilt of self-pity and irrelevant thoughts, such as; I wonder what Ping will cook for dinner tonight; that car across from me is full of Somalian men and I hope they don't shoot me; I think the Jays are starting their season soon; and then, I wonder if I'm going to go to jail.

Damnit, that's not irrelevant enough!

Before I realize what I'm doing, I find the steering wheel guiding me towards the exit for my house (or the burned-up patch of land where my house used to sit). I take the exit for Innes Road and curl around the curved underpass, stopping at the same lights I've stopped at a thousand times before, although, there is a refreshing sense of unfamiliarity this time as I sit waiting for the light to change.

There have been reports of a young girl...

I methodically make it to my street and pull up beside the charred remains of what used to be my home. I park my car at the edge of the lawn beside my mailbox and sit there comatose behind the wheel, staring at my own hands as the sound of static echoes inside my skull. Taking a deep breath, I push open the car door with considerable effort and step outside into the evening air. The sun hangs low in the sky as a chilled wind sends a shiver down my spine, while soft whispers echo inside my mind.

I begin to move towards the ruble which has been taped off lazily with yellow caution. I take faint notice that the little red flag on the mailbox has been flipped up.

If a house burns down but the mailbox remains...

I open the mailbox and find a bundle of envelopes waiting to great me. I can't help but laugh as I scoop out the overdue bill notices, chucking them haphazardly onto the lawn in a scattered pile. I can picture the mailman, just another cog in the bureaucratic machine, walking on by my burned down house, not even bothering to notice that it's been reduced to nothing but ash, and casually slipping my mortgage bill into the mailbox...

Does anybody notice anything anymore?

I saunter over closer to the crime scene (the culprit always returns to the scene of the crime), stepping over burned chards of what used to be part of my liquid assets, and feeling remarkably little for the loss. I come to the edge of where my house used to stand, and somehow, probably through sheer instinct and habit, I find myself standing exactly where my front door used to be. There are chunks of brick and wood still intact, everything blackened, I can see a half-burned chair sitting where my kitchen was, and it looks incredibly lonely standing there amongst the ruble. There are still plumes of smoke rising from pockets of debris, and a sour smell fills my nostrils as I continue to scan my burned-up life.

And then I see her.

Standing there in the middle of the ruble, barefooted, wearing a stained brown dress, her pale arms hanging down by her sides, and long dark hair covering her face. I look around, hoping to find a neighbour in the vicinity, but there is no one, the street is completely dead. A gust of wind lifts the shirt off my back and I can hear my heart beating inside my head.

She sees me.

She knows me.

She takes a step forward. And then another. I stand my ground, acutely aware that I have most certainly descended into complete madness.

"Are you happy?" I call out to her. "Are you happy now that I've ruined it all?"

She peers through her long strands of black hair, with eyes all red and burning.

"I'm sorry," I say, as she moves ever closer, only a few feet away now, he could see her eyes beneath the strands of hair, like two black marbles forced inside her head. "I never meant... I didn't want... you know, I would have loved to have a daughter, now that I think about it. Truly. I would have loved you, and I'll have to live with that for the rest of my life, the fact that I was hoping... for, well, I don't really know exactly what I was hoping for... that's the problem with men, you know? We never think things through... and it's true, you would have bankrupted me, I'm quite sure of it, but still, I don't think I would have minded so much, certainly, I'd be happier than I am now..."

She shakes her head, standing directly in front of me now, and reaching out with her skeleton fingers, her skin seemingly translucent in the sunlight, she places her cold palm upon my shoulder, leaning forward and pulling me close, she lets out raspy cough as her jaw detaches with a sickening crack, her mouth a gaping hole, and I watch with growing anxiety as a giant beetle the size of a basketball starts pulling itself from her mouth.

"Jesus Fucking Christ!" I stumble backwards, almost losing my footing.

"Mark?"

Whirling around in tremendous fashion, I find my neighbour, Brian, or Steve, or whatever the fuck his name is, standing at the edge of his lawn, looking over at me with his hands on his hips, his head cocked in the same way Maximus used to look at me when I came home late from the strip club stinking of booze and stale vagina.

"You okay?" he asks.

"Oh yeah," I say, standing straight up and turning sharply towards him like a soldier who has just been commanded to About Face.

"Who were you talking to just now?"

Turning my head, I see that my dead daughter's ghost has vanished, evaporating into thin air, and I look back towards my neighbour, offering him a confused shrug and nothing more. I make the long walk across the lawn towards my car, while Brian-Steve-Whateverthefuck watches me with raised eyebrows.

"I'm sorry about your house," he calls after me. "Let us know if there's anything..."

"Yeah, yeah," I say, waving my hand at him as I dash into my car. "Thanks for your concern," I call out to him before shutting the car door. "You always were a good neighbour!"

I'm in my father's guest room which is on the first floor beside the kitchen, lying on the tiny guest bed (rather than passing out drunkenly on the couch, again), with one hand gripped firmly around my testicles, feeling and prodding them, attempting to pinpoint the time in my life when I was at my most content. That ever elusive 'happiest moment' that seems to always slip through the cracks of the average person's life. It happens, passes, and then we don't realize it until we are filling up little hanging plastic bags with shit and piss on our deathbeds.

Was it that first year Trace and I met in University? When we fucked two times a day (minimum), smoked cigarettes together in bed, or sitting on the windowsill together, our naked bodies intertwined in that obnoxious way of new lovers, the moonlight flitting in through the parted curtains as I played with her breasts with my free hand.

Or was it before then, when I was in high school? Playing hockey and basketball and drinking at bush parties and losing my virginity to Stacy Plainview (and boy was she plain!). Those days of complete and utter disregard for responsibility; those days of unprovoked freedom that so many of us allow to slide on by without really taking stock of just how rare that sort of freedom is.

Or was it when Thomas was born (before I turned him into a frantic bleeding-heart liberal)? I remember staying up late with him, rocking him in my arms when he was merely the size of a small watermelon, walking back and forth in our living room making strange cooing sounds and other sorts of crazy noises parents make to their newborn children.

Sighing, I let my eyes wander about the mostly empty room. No one ever put any effort into their guest rooms. Everything was always so bland. A bed that's too small, a worn out and discarded night table, a weird old lamp that has the old-fashioned twisty switch hidden somewhere beneath the lampshade, walls bare, maybe a chair if you're lucky, a closet that is either empty or full of all the outdated and undersized clothing from a past life, and maybe a pile of well-read novels tucked in the back corner on the floor.

I would rather be a bathroom than a guest room. At least people took pride in their bathrooms.

My fingers fall upon the bulge in my right testicle, all grotesque and misshapen, and it hurts when I squeeze it.

Fucking cancer.

My phone starts vibrating beside me in bed, and I don't have to check the caller ID to know that it's Trace. She'd been phoning nonstop all day, but since my Voicemail is full, I haven't had the pleasure of hearing what new development has got her in a telephone frenzy. I can safely assume the police have contacted her at this point, and I can only imagine what sort of thoughts went through Tracy's mind when the cops brought up siting a young woman around the property. I am undoubtedly certain that she's going to assume its Cheryl.

Shit that's not a bad idea, you know. You could always try to put the frame on Cheryl... she certainly acted insane enough over the past week to justify that sort of action...

"Shut-up," I say out loud to the empty room, addressing my own conscience. "You've made enough trouble for us as it is."

Hey don't blame me, you know, I wouldn't exist without you.

"Yeah, thanks for reminding me."

Hey, at least you'll never be able to have kids again!

But this thought, a thought which would have once brought me sincere joy and gratitude, fills me with a strange sort of longing that leaves me feeling slightly less human than before, if that were possible.

The thought of jerking off crosses my mind, and although I try to dismiss it, I can't help but think that it's probably the best thing I can do at the moment, given the circumstances.

May as well enjoy my testicle while I still can.

Wednesday

I awake to the buzzing of my phone. It's Trace. I reach for it with trembling fingers, my head a little fuzzy from the rum I drank late last night after failing to fall asleep, but my hand pauses in midair as I am reaching for it, as if controlled by some invisible string. I let the call go to voice mail, and proceed to lie there staring at the phone as if I'm half expecting it to grow legs.

The bare walls of my father's guest room greet me as I force myself from the bed, yawning and scratching at my armpits. I can hear someone click-clacking in the kitchen and find my father over the oven as I exit the guestroom.

"Morning Mark," he says, "Eggs?"

"No, I don't think so," I sigh. "Haven't had much of an appetite lately."

"Stress can do that to a man's stomach."

I go over to the couch in the living room, collapsing upon it like a top-heavy crane tipping over. I rub my eyes and sigh, staring at the white ceiling and wondering just what in the hell I am going to do with myself. The fact that my house is gone, as well as my wife, is finally beginning to dawn on me, like an anchor that spent the last few days floating in the water has finally sunk all the way to the bottom of the ocean, coming to a slamming thud against the cold earth below.

"You look like a man whose mind has betrayed him."

I am startled from my reverie to find my father standing over me, his arms crossed loosely in front of his belly.

"Maybe you should get some air, go for a walk or something."

"Sounds reasonable."

"I'm a reasonable man."

I get my ass up from the couch and throw on a flannel jacket. The sun is shining outside and a light breeze propels me down my father's long gravel driveway. I get out to the road and take a left, where there's another quick turn to the right, and then I'm walking down a seemingly endless road carved between the trees. For the first time in a long time, I feel like I can actually breathe. There is something about being in a place where the trees outnumbered people...

Trace would like this...

And my heart swells as the sun creeps through the tree branches. I can feel the tiny hole, burning at the centre, like a crater filled with fire, and I wonder if I'm going to die alone. Death would be such a sweet release at this point. My feet drag upon the gravel, a car drives by, a bird chirps somewhere above, and all of it passes through me like water through a bottomless glass. I've lost my foundation. I no longer know who I am, which is liberating in a horrifying and lonely sort of way. How did I ever let it come to this? To allow my life to slip away oh-so-gradually to the point where I can't remember the last time I was truly happy (and no, burning my house down doesn't count).

I know she's following me. I've felt her presence for the past few kilometres, but I'm too afraid to turn around. I can hear her footfalls scraping along the pavement, and her heavy breath, scraping against her throat.

I killed my daughter.

With my thoughts. With my deeds. With my intentions. I am a murderer.

Thomas's face flashes through my mind, that same face he gave me in the hospital waiting room, of pure and utter disgust, and I suppose I deserved that look, and this thought only perpetuates the guilt that I have for the fact that after nineteen years I still have no fucking clue who my son is or what he is all about. The only thing I know for sure is that he hates me, and I cannot blame him for that.

Trace...

198

We were so close. So close to redemption, I could almost taste it. But that's life, isn't it? The most fleeting of moments filled with hope, quickly swallowed by the gaping abyss of reality which comes on too fast and too strong for you to deal with.

On the horizon, I see a steeple reaching into the sky above the tree line, the cross beckoning me forth like a pointed finger. I try to remember the last time I stepped foot in a church. It must have been ten years ago, when we took Helen to church on Christmas Eve, when Thomas was still a chubby boy without a clue and still listened to the words I said as if they were gospel. When he would nod his head rather than roll his eyes.

Do you love your son?

Yes.

Are you sure?

It's not about being sure, it's just the way it is.

Sounds like an arbitrary obligation. But do you love him?

What the fuck is love, anyways? Is it sacrifice? Is it longing? Is it fear? Probably all of those things. Love is an addiction. That's probably the best way to put it.

As I pass the entrance to the church, I pause, staring at the door like a long-lost friend.

Fuck it. I make my way to the hulking wooden doors and push. That familiar smell hits me, old wood mixed with faint scents of candles and wine.

I enter the church vestibule and pause, struck by the red carpeting and red velvet ropes that hang from the walls. There is a giant stained-glass window of the Virgin Mother, her placid face looking down upon me, her eyes like giant blue diamonds glittering in the light. Poor Mary, all the pain and none of the pleasure. She truly was a saint for agreeing to such barbarous terms.

I sigh and move through the giant oak doors and into the nave of the cathedral. It is a tiny church, with two rows of pews stretching ten deep. The wooden benches are covered with red cushions, and the tall but thin stained-glass windows display the various saints and apostles, their noble and righteous noses pointed high in the air.

199

"A lot of good you guys did when it really mattered," I mutter to myself, taking a seat in the back row and coughing as the dust from the red cushion plumes all around me.

The alter stands benevolent at the front centre, a giant cross hung directly behind it. There is a wreath of red roses placed off to the side on a stand, and I wonder whose death they are supposed to represent. Whenever I saw flowers in a church, I always assumed they were there to represent death.

I close my eyes and try to feel something, anything, kneeling down upon the floor with my hands clasped together over the back of the bench in front of me, as I had been taught to do back in Sunday School when church still seemed like a very important and scary thing to me. Back when believing in a fella named Jesus was not only fashionable, but fathomable. The very idea that a man could be so selfless and so forgiving was a dubious notion in my mind, to say the least. The only truth about the bible that I ever saw, was the fact that in the end, everyone will betray you. Humanity will ultimately let you down.

"Can I help you, my son?"

"Jesus Christ!" I cry, jerking forward and slamming my knee off the back of the pew. "Fuck!"

The priest stares back at me with wide, searching eyes, his pupils scanning me up and down, side to side, trying to decipher whether I pose any sort of threat. He is standing at the end of the pew, his wrinkled hand clasped upon the edge of the back bench.

"Sorry," I say, stammering. "I, you know... well, you should never take the Lord's name in vain, right?"

"Quite right," he nods. "Now, is there something I can do for you? You look lost."

He is an older man, bald with a white beard. His black robes hang from his body in loose wrinkles, and the wrinkles which line his face and hands are pronounced, although his eyes possessed a striking liveliness. They were a deep shade of green that almost seemed to glow in the dim lighting of the church, and they were always moving, studying, it seemed.

"I'm not sure..."

"A man has questions."

"Well, yeah, I mean, who doesn't?"

"You are wondering what has brought you here?"

"The road, I suppose."

"And which road is this?"

"Pretty sure it's Highway 7..."

"What about your road?" he asks me, his eyes forever locking with mine. I had yet to see him blink.

"My road?" I laugh. "Look, I just came in here to sit down, to see if maybe... I don't know, to see if maybe I could feel something."

"And did you?"

"Loneliness," I tell him. "It only made me feel lonely."

"Perhaps you are angry with God for failing to answer your prayers?"

"I haven't been really keeping up with my prayers, Father. If I'm being completely honest with yah."

"It's never to late to start."

"Ah, sometimes it is though. Like when a tumor is allowed to grow inside you. Eventually it gets to a point where there's nothing that can be done, nothing that will completely erase it, you know? I'm terminally ill, you see Father? And I don't think there's any sort of medication that will fix me."

"May I ask you, my son, when was the last time you partook in confession?"

"Ah," I sigh, suddenly feeling quite suffocated. "I was afraid you might ask that."

"Has it been that long?" he asks, his eyebrows raised.

"Oh, it's not about that," I say. "It's just the fact that I think the whole act of confession, this whole idea of admitting to your faults and repenting, it just seems like a giant crock of shit to me, to be honest, and if anything, it only works to justify and rationalize further sinful behaviour, because I mean, if god is going to forgive me anyways so long as I say sorry, then fuck it, right? May as well rape and pillage and kill while I can, and spend my later years repenting for it, you know?"

The priest stares at me stunned, his eyes suddenly far less

201

colourful, and he shuffles away from me then, opening up an escape route for me at the end of the pew. I make my way there and start for the door, but I stop suddenly, turning back and calling out to the priest. He pauses and turns to face me slowly, his lips pulled back and face tilted upward in stoic sincerity.

"Are ghosts real?"

"But of course," he nods. "They live on through us, you see, these demons birthed by our own wretched sins."

And with that, the old man turns from me again and walks back towards the chancel, his feet shuffling upon the red carpet in soft whispers, and I can picture myself hung up above the alter, nails through my wrists and feet, and I can't help but wish that I'd dropped those twenty pounds I promised myself I would after the New Year. Goddamn you, social expectations; even in my moments of enlightenment, you end up making me feel fat.

On my way back to the house, I get a text from Jim.

Mark, I'm in trouble. I need your help.

I try calling him but his phone goes straight to voicemail.

"Goddamnit Jim..." I sigh, wondering how on earth I can be expected to stay sober when my AA sponsor is a goddamn train wreck.

I pick up my pace as the sun begins its slow descent. A gust of wind sweeps up from behind, propelling me forward and causing the trees to sway, the branches scratching at each other like battling brooms.

I pass by a dead crow on the side of the road, it's tiny black legs pointed towards the sky like abandoned flag poles. It's black eyes seem to follow me as I make my way gingerly past, giving the deceased bird a wide birth, and as the sun begins to dip below the treeline, the shadows running longer now, growing drastically in the dim light like grotesque mutants, and I can see my silhouette on the pavement, a long thin figure, emancipated.

I decide to stop by Jim's place before the meeting, dreading to find him in a similar state as the last time. For the love of god, please at least allow him to have made it to the bathroom this time. There was something about the smell of stale urine that lingered. It stuck with you even after leaving the room, if you now what I mean.

There is a man with a shaved head standing out front of the apartment building wearing a leather vest and a battered pair of blue jeans. His arms are crossed in front of his chest and I do my best to avoid his eyes as I approach the entranceway, his eyes following me with every step, and I take faint notice of the many skull tattoos covering his forearms. I can feel his eyes all hot on the back of my neck as I buzz Jim's apartment, teetering back and forth on my heels with my hands in my pockets. I realize that I'm humming to myself and put an abrupt end to the chorus. After a dozen rings the line goes dead and a robotic voice tells me to hang up and try again. I pull out my phone and try calling him, but the voicemail picks up after one ring, asking me to please leave my name and number at the beep.

"Fuck," I whisper. Looking around aimlessly at the mostly empty street. Ottawa could be a very quiet city sometimes, even when you were downtown on a Wednesday afternoon. Bureaucrats prefer the anonymity and reclusiveness of dark and damp places, so I've been told. Sometimes I liked to picture them working down in the sewers, a bunch of green skinned mutants, typing away on their laptop computers as they repeatedly request further documentation and proof of identity.

"You looking for Jim?"

I whirl around in tremendous fashion, nearly whacking my hand against the guy's chest in the process. The man with the shaved head has crept up behind me and is standing about a foot away from my face.

"Jim?"

"Yeah, I'm looking for Jim too."

"Oh, I'm not here for Jim. Don't know anyone named Jim, in fact."

"Is that right?" he asks, scratching at his chin, the dried skin sounding like sandpaper beneath his fingernails. "Seems kinda funny though, since I watched you dial his buzzer number."

"Look buddy, I don't know what to tell yah, alright?"

I shrug and brush past him, making my way quickly back to the car. I keep an eye on the pavement for his shadow to creep up form behind me, but it never comes. I basically lunge into the driver's side seat and peel out from the sidewalk with a screech of the tires, the man with the shaved head observing me the entire time, a tight little grin etched across his face, and I can feel a sinking pit in my stomach as I attempt to call Jim again. Same result, right to voicemail.

On my way to AA I get another call from Doctor Von Haymen, which I promptly ignore. I get a little notification telling me that my voicemail is currently full, which suits me just fine since that prevents anyone from leaving me further messages asking for payments or blood work.

I pull into the parking lot and search for Jim's beaten up corvette. It's not here.

"Fuck," I whisper to myself.

I make my way towards the gymnasium doors, and suddenly I come to the grim realization that I am in fact sober.

Why are you even here, Marky boy?

And this thought flitters through my mind like a bird's wings, all flapping and gusting, and I can't quite explain why it is I've continued to attend the meetings, because in all honesty, I'm not even sure myself. It's almost as if I've been doing it out of habit, you know? Subconsciously or some shit. Because this is the first time I've even thought about the fact that I am no longer required to be here.

Well, turn the fuck around then.

But I keep moving forward, my feet propelling me towards the doors like a car with no brakes.

I find myself a seat near the back row of chairs, as usual, and sit there scanning the room for Jim. Goddamnit, he's not here. He's sitting in that shithole of an apartment rubbing his goddamn chaffed nose and smoking darts. And this thought fills me with a sick sort of dread as I contemplate what a responsible and good person would do if their friend was in such a situation.

"Good evening everyone," Tony says at the front. "Let's jump right into it. Is there anyone who would like to share?"

And before I can stop myself, I am up on my feet, walking towards the front with an outstretched hand.

Mark, what the fuck are you doing? Sit the fuck back down!

But it's too late now, because I've got the mic in my hand and I'm staring down at all my companions here in this brightly lit gymnasium. Time to lay it all on the line, Marky boy. Time to finally confess your sins to the world. And sure, maybe I'm simply seeking absolution, or maybe, just maybe, I'm actually trying to change.

"My name is Markus, and I'm not an alcoholic."

There's a low rumbling that sweeps over the crowd, people shaking their heads and coughing, and I see the head guy begin to move towards me, his eyes narrowed and mouth drawn back in a thin line.

"I'm not an alcoholic," I say again, "because I don't deserve that title. I can't be an alcoholic if I'm not human, right? I'm not worthy to be associated with the human condition. I am everything that is wrong with our society. Selfish. Self-entitled. Spoiled. I'm the guy who relishes in your failures. I'm the one who laughs at your pain. Like red wine, I leave a stain."

"I'm the asshole who snickers behind your back in public, and laughs right in your fucking face in private. I'm the guy who will yell at the young waitress at the countryside diner for not getting my order right. I'm the guy who sends his food back sometimes just for fun, you know? Just to be a dick. To show that I can."

"I allow myself to think simple-minded thoughts and make gross generalizations because it's easier that way. I never became the man my nineteen-year-old self thought I was going to be, and since the day I realized that, I guess I've been sort of bitter and pissed off about it, like I'm trying to get revenge on the world, or maybe myself... I'm not even sure, all I know is that I'm a cynical miserable piece of shit."

"Worse yet, I am an intolerant man. I blame others for my problems while having no sympathy for the problems of others. It's like there's a hole in my heart... or a vacuum, I guess, and all my emotions get sucked up into a single ball of self-pity and jealousy. At the end of the day, I'm just a selfish, bitter old man. I read somewhere that victimhood is the first step towards fascism, and I guess I understand what that means now... irrational thought. It infects the mind like a virus, it spreads..."

"I'm the man who neglects his family and then blames them for it. I make up excuses as to why I don't know my son, or why I have been unfaithful to my wife. I tell myself it's their fault. I pretend that I don't care in order to mask the giant lump of guilt that sits forever in my throat. All these sweet little lies bundled up to create a rotting bouquet of hope. To create the illusion of family, of love. I cannot remember the last time I did something truly generous without some sort of ulterior motive. Self-grandeur, appeasement, rationalization. Whatever the true motive is, I can fucking guarantee you it's not generosity."

"And lately I've been seeing my dead daughter following me around. And she's older than she ever got to be, I mean, her ghost is. Her ghost is older than she would have been, so that means the ghost actually lived longer than my daughter, you know what I mean?"

I can tell by their puzzled faces that they in fact do not know what I mean.

"It's just... I feel... really sad... but no, its not sadness. Not really. It's more like guilt. I feel guilty for letting my family down, time and time again. And its not even the booze, although that certainly didn't help. It's more than that. I'm... I've failed to be a man. I should have taken things more seriously... tried to enjoy the time I had, but instead I just spent my whole life finding one reason after another not to be happy... one more reason to drink a bottle of rye and forget about my so-called problems..."

"Your life's not over yet, Mark!"

And that fact that he knows my name, this faceless man in the crowd, stirs something in me that causes me to choke up. I try to continue but I cannot, and as I move away from the mic, a single person starts clapping, and by the time I get to my seat, everyone in the gym is standing and clapping and nodding at me, and you know what, Jesus fucking Christ it did actually makes me feel a bit better.

I get back to my seat and sit down, attempting to settle this bubbling feeling of achievement inside my stomach. Certainly, I felt a considerable weight lifted from my shoulders, and yet there was still a gnawing feeling in the back of my mind, telling me that this is simply the beginning...

I wish Jim was here to see this.

My phone vibrates and beeps so I pull it out and see a text message from Jim. I open up the message and read the five simple words spelled out in all capital letters.

COME NOW OR JIM GETS IT.

I pull up to Jim's apartment and park the car against the sidewalk in front, slamming my wheel against the curb in the process. I can hear the man's voice echoing in my ears. Come now, OR JIM GETS IT.

Jesus Jim, what did you get yourself into?

None of this feels real.

I come to the front of the apartment and stand there motionless for a moment, adrenaline surging through my veins, I can feel my heart beating against the corner of my head, and I take a deep breath as I massage my temples. Get your shit together, Mark.

I pull out my phone and dial Jim's number. It rings twice before he answers.

"Buzz up," a gruff and unfamiliar voice demands, ending the call with a beep.

I punch in the ringer and wait for the harsh buzz to let me in. The buzz comes and I open the door, my mind still racing.

I should have grabbed a weapon.

Oh yeah? And what would you have done with it, tough guy? The last physical confrontation you got into was with yourself in the shower when you slipped and fell against your own fat gut.

I climb the three flights of stairs and enter the hallway.

Having a weapon would only increase your likelihood of getting killed.

And this last thought seems to ring true enough, and so I make my way towards Jim's door and stop facing it. I can hear heavy breathing coming from the other side. Muffled sounds of scuffling.

The door flings open and, in a flash, I am flung inside, stumbling and falling on my fat useless ass. The man with the shaved head stands over me, the gun in his hand clearly visible, and I stare into his glaring eyes, wondering if this is perhaps the place I die. On the floor of my AA sponsor's shithole one-bedroom apartment. Seems fitting enough, I suppose.

"Hello again," he says. "You Jim's buddy or something?"

"He's my sponsor."

The man with the shaved head studies me as he attempts to determine whether I am serious or not. At some point, he realizes it doesn't matter and drags me into the living room, where Jim is sprawled out on the couch, his face a bloody mess, nose clearly broken. He looks at me all wide eyed and frantic, and as he tries to say something he begins to cough, choking on his own blood. The man with the shaved head shoves me against the wall and slugs me in the gut, leaving me all hunched over and heaving. As I fight to regain my composure, I see there's cocaine spilled all over the coffee table, cigarette butts scattered all over the floor from an upturned ashtray. The sound of Jim attempting to breathe through his rattling nostrils fills me with a foreboding dread that I cannot quite explain. It was as if thousands of tiny insects were attempting to crawl out from under my skin. A sinking sort of feeling that leaves me gasping for air as Jim mumbles half broken apologizes through his mangled face.

"Shut the fuck up, Jim," the shaved headed man says. "So, you got the money?"

"Money?" I ask, on the verge of laughter.

"Yeah, the money your buddy owes me."

"Sorry man, no money... my house just burned down to be honest, and my wife is leaving me..."

"I don't give a shit!" he screams, brandishing the pistol. "Who's got my fucking money?"

"How much are we talking here?"

"Ten grand."

"Oh Jim," I say, sighing. "What the fuck..."

"You know what?" the man with the shaved head says, letting

his shoulders slack as his eyes shift from Jim to me, and for a moment, I am actually able to convince myself that he is giving up. That he is going to simply shrug his shoulders and walk on out of Jim's apartment.

And that's when the pistol strikes me in the side of the face. I hit the ground hard, and feel my warm blood soaking the left side of my face, like a hot wave.

"I'm sick of this shit!" the man with the shaved head screams, kicking me repeatedly in the ribs. I cannot catch my breath, and I instinctively bring my arms up to protect my face.

The assault stops momentarily, and I risk looking up at my assailant, who stands over me with a face glowing red, the violent rise and fall of his chest matches the contempt in his tiny eyes, and he cocks his pistol then, staring down at me with malevolence.

"You really wanna die for this scumbag?" he asks. "Just give me the money and I'll let you both live."

"I don't have any fucking money," I say, and without being able to control myself, I begin to laugh. "I don't have a fucking thing, man. My life is a fucking joke. I've got nothing left. Nothing material anyway, which is perfectly fine with me since I don't have a single goddamn person who I could share it with. So, what are we really doing here, huh? If you want to know the truth, the God's honest truth," I pause, letting the laughter explode from my crippled body in harsh waves, pain shooting up the side of my body and a pulsing sort of ache in the side of my face. The man with the shaved head stares down at me with a fascinated sort of contempt, breathing heavily.

"You'd be doing me a fucking favour," I tell him, still unable to stifle the bursts of deranged giggles that escape from my chest. "Do it! Put that gun to my head and pull the fucking trigger. It's a more admirable exit than I deserve, to be honest. And frankly, I don't give a fucking shit anymore, and I'm certainly not going to lie here begging for my life to some two-bit drug dealing thug who thinks...."

His foot connects with my jaw in a sickening crunch. I feel the broken bone poking against the inside of my cheek, and the taste of blood fills my mouth in a sickening rush. Tastes like metal.

"Well, I wasn't going to fucking kill you, bucko," he says, pausing to spit on me like the goddamn gentleman he is. "But you've convinced me."

And as he's pointing the gun at my head, I can feel my consciousness begin to slip, fading behind the blackness, a dream, just a dream, and I hear Jim's muffled cry as the door to the apartment bursts open, and just before everything goes completely black, I see Mister Officer Sir rushing inside with his gun drawn, and the deafening sounds of the shots ring out inside my skull as I sink beneath the fog, my mind finally slipping away, away from all of this, away from all the pain, but most of all, away from myself.

Hospital

Lights flicker in and out, behind my eyelids there are shadows dancing, arms reaching, and a soft whispering call that seems to go on and on, even after the shadows have left.

Hands reaching over me... the clank-clank-clank of metallic instruments. There's a tunnel of light blinding me, and inside the sphere I can see shapes and colours swirling, like a rainbow tornado inside my skull, I have the feeling of floating... soft whispers with concerned tones, a voice saying my name over and over again; Markus, Markus, Markus. Where am I? It was hard to say. Did I get shot? Am I dying? It was impossible to tell. And in this obliviousness, I can see my daughter's face, or what her face may have looked like if she would have survived, and she's smiling at me with a gaping, toothless grin, laughing frantically as her eyes do summersaults in their sockets. Daddy, daddy, daddy! What have you done? Were you trying to impress me, daddy? Showing off a bit, eh old man? Where you trying to make it up to me? Well, I'm sorry to say, there's nothing to make up, because I'm dead, daddy. I've always been dead.

There's a ringing sound that morphs into a steady high-pitched tone. It continues on infinitely inside my head as the colours continue to swirl.

I can hear the odd beep, and I wonder how close to death I am. If perhaps I had already died. It was very hard to tell, sort of like swimming through a cloud, it was impossible to tell whether you were closer to the sky or the ground.

Only that you are floating.

I come to long enough to establish that I am still in fact alive, which is good, I guess. I can hear the doctor muttering something in medical jargon to an unseen nurse. The scratch of a pencil on a clipboard (hospitals must be one of the last bastions for pencil salesmen), and then silence. After a while the humming comes back and it soothes me so that I can pass out again.

Back to the cloud.

Back to floating.

I am no one.

I am nothing.

I awake in the middle of the night in a cold sweat. I pass through the frantic moment of wondering where the hell I am and move right into the oh-my-god-what-the-fuck-happened-to-my-face mode. I can tell my nose has been bandaged on account of not being able to breathe through it. I touch at the top of it gently, and for my troubles, I am greeted by a sharp flare of pain which explodes up into my eyes and causes me to gasp, which only results in further pain exploding from my broken jaw.

I can still open my mouth about a half an inch to suck air, but other than that, my whole face appears to be stapled together.

It's at this point I notice the cast on my right arm and remember the exact moment when the shaved headed bastard broke it with his fat fucking foot.

I sigh and realize that my other hand is grasped firmly around a long slender device with a red button on the end of it which I instantly recognize (thanks to my wife's obsession with Gray's Anatomy) as the morphine button. I press it repeatedly until I pass out, a slight smile drawn upon my broken face.

"Markus."

Her voice. Swimming up towards her voice.

I open my eyes to find Trace sitting beside my bed, her hand placed upon my chest, and her face breaks as I smile up at her and say it'shoo good to shee you, baby.

"Oh Markus!" she cries. "What did you go and get yourself wrapped up in?"

"Yer no mee," I manage to slur together. A hot white flash of pain flashes up my cheek and into my temple, and I cringe noticeably, causing Trace to make a high-pitched coo and proceed to tenderly brush my hair.

"I was so mad at you..."

I feel my face redden and I try to suppress the tears welling up, but considering I can't really move my face much, they start pouring out over the edges of my eyelids, and for the first time in a long time, I realize just what a lucky bastard I am, and just how inconceivably stupid I have behaved over the past decade or so.

"I sowy," I say.

My wife looks down at me, and I see a grin creep across her face. "You know you just sounded exactly like Ping, right?"

It takes a moment to sink in, but before I can stop it or control it, Trace and I are both howling with laughter, and I can feel the pins in my jaw clanking around, tears stream down my cheeks in hot torrents, but I cannot stop myself from laughing.

A nurse comes rushing in and scolds Trace and I with her eyes, all squinted and suspicious.

"He shouldn't be laughing," she says, coming over and checking something on one of the monitors beeping around me.

"Yes, well, as you get to know my husband, you will come to realize that he often does things that he should not."

The nurse gives Trace a glance that screams this is no laughing matter, and scowls at us as she makes her exit, swinging her arms around like the proper mechanical asshole that she is.

The two of us sit in silence for a moment, my wife staring at me with her eyes as big as stars, sparkling like tiny diamonds encased within the most precious of containers. How have I been so oblivious?

"Do you remember, back in university, when I used to make you give me rides?"

"Yers, ofe course."

"You'd get down on all fours and crawl around that shitty little apartment of yours with me on your back..."

I swallow down the lump in my throat, my eyes betraying me.

"And do you remember the time when we were hammered back in university. I was mad at you... I think I caught you doing coke or something, and we were walking down Bank Street, and after I told that group of bums to fuck off, you grabbed me and we slipped on the ice, and I fell backwards and would have definitely smashed my head off the pavement, but you shielded me with your arms, and I remember your elbow swelled up something terrible the next day, but you saved me Markus, you protected me....

"I'm sowy I stropped..."

"You know I have to leave you, right?"

"Yers-I-no."

"But I will always love you, Mark. I hope you know that as well. I do." She smiles then and leans over me, kissing me softly on the lips, and then she makes for the door before the sobs can completely take hold, but just before she reaches it, something stops her.

"Oh, I almost forgot to tell you," she says, turning back towards me, wiping her tear stained cheeks. "I'm getting published!"

"No shit."

"Yup," she says smiling. "Love has no Language."

"Ofe course."

"And there's one more thing," she says. "I met someone... online. We're going on our first date tomorrow night..."

"I knew Facebook was a bad idea."

Just then, Doctor Von Haymen comes bursting into the room, nearly bowling over my wife in the process.

"So sorry!" he says, clutching his clipboard and adjusting his thick rimmed glasses upon his nose. He is a short man with bushy eyebrows and fat lips. "But I've been meaning to get a hold of Mark for the past few days. He does have quite a nasty habit of disappearing when things are indeed at their most crucial point..."

"You can say that again," my wife laughs, winking at me. "I guess I'll leave you two to it..."

"Actually, Mrs. Stanfield, you should probably stay for this."

My wife looks at Doctor Von Haymen quizzically, her face all scrunched up like a mouse whose just taken a whiff of some rotten cheese.

"Mark, as you know, we diagnosed you with testicular cancer last time you were here..."

"Yesh, I do sheem to recall..."

"Well, as often happens, there can be misdiagnoses, especially when it comes to sensitive areas such as the testicles, and so I'm here with good news... you do not, in fact, have cancer."

"Praish Jeshush!" I exclaim, my jaw burning with a pain that I am far too relieved to bother acknowledging.

Trace runs to me and gives me a big hug, causing further pain to shoot up the entire side of my torso.

"Yes, what we initially thought was a cancerous tumor has actually revealed itself to be nothing more than a symptom of syphilitis..."

"Syphilitis?"

"Yes, commonly known as syphilis."

Eureka!

"Obviously, Mrs. Stanfield, you'll want to be tested and treated if you and your husband have engaged in any form of intercourse over the past year... which, clearly you have so... perhaps you'd like to follow me to an examination room where we can extract some blood..."

"Un-fuckin-believable," Trace says, looking down at me with burning eyes. "Without fail, you have a way of spoiling even the most tender moments. You really are a walking disaster, you know it Mark?"

"I'm aware."

Trace sighs and says let's go then to the Doctor, and the two of them leave me to stew in these new revelations, and although I should likely be experiencing some sort of existential moment of relief, regret, guilt and shame, I decide it's probably easier to simply press the little red button again and sink beneath the tides of morphine drips. Fuck you Cancer! And thank god for syphilis.

"You're a lucky man, Mr. Stanfield."

I come swimming from my subconscious in a slow crawl, the familiar voice of Mister Officer Sir echoing in my ears. He stands over my bed in his navy-blue uniform, staring down at me with his goddamn sunglasses on. I can see my own reflection in the black lenses, and what I see horrifies me. My one eye is practically swollen shut, all yellow and black, and there is a fresh gash on the side of my face from where the man's pistol came crashing against it. My nose is heavily bandaged and my jaw has lumps on its left side that are sickening. I look away at this point for fear that I may vomit.

"It's a good thing I was having you surveilled," Mister Officer Sir continues, "otherwise this could have turned out much differently for you and your friend."

"Heesh-not-my-friend, heesh-my-sponsor," I manage to mumble.

"That guy was your AA sponsor?" the cop says, shaking his head. "Jesus Christ."

He looks down at me then in all seriousness, his mouth pulling back into a thin line.

"Why didn't you call the cops?" he asks me.

"Oh, I don't know. I shuppose I wanted to be the hero for one-sh..."

"Well," he says, looking me over, "You certainly seemed to have suffered enough for one day..." he pauses. "Look, I'll drop the investigation on you, but I want to hear it. I want you to tell me you burned your own house down."

"I burned my housh down."

"And why exactly did you do that, if I may ask?"

"I guesh I jusht wanted to watch the flame-sh," I say, my jaw aching with every syllable.

Mister Officer Sir sighs and shakes his head. "You know what I don't get?" And even though I do not acknowledge his question, he steam rolls on through anyways. "I've seen your type before you know. Middle aged man, family, good job... and for some reason, you idiots seem to go out of your way to destroy everything in your lives... it's like you're asking for it. Like the pressure of having a good life is too much for you to bare, and so you create problems for yourselves... it's like you're bored or something, and maybe you are bored, but that doesn't change the fact that you are

216

also blind. Blind to the blessings and the good graces you have been afforded. And it's the blindness that pisses me off the most, because guess what, Mark, you have a good life. You have the potential to be a good man. So why don't you just wake the fuck up and start acting accordingly?"

With that, Mister Officer Sir turns from my bed and exits the room, not bothering to look back before leaving, and I am left yet again to stew, staring at the door and wondering if I should be devastated or grateful. I hit the morphine button and decide it doesn't matter, not for now. Only the fog. Take me back beneath the fog where I can swim amongst my delusions, dancing beneath the darkness like bats flapping through the night.

I awake to my son sitting beside my bed, his eyebrow ring glinting in the incandescent light. I wonder briefly if perhaps I have died and am currently being subjected to some sort of perverted purgatory, forced to face an endless stream of people in my life who I've let down time and time again. It would certainly be a fitting punishment.

The hot-bright pain in my jaw confirms that I am indeed still alive.

"Hey, you're awake."

"Mmmmmyeah." I manage to mumble. My jaw is stiff and sore and it feels like there's a bee inside my cheek that is repeatedly stinging me, a throbbing sort of itch that's impossible to extinguish, sort of like the guilty worm writhing within my belly.

"How are you feeling?"

I shrug, mumble incoherent syllables, and watch my son frown. He's wearing a tightly fitted flannel long-sleeved shirt with some black jeans that I doubt Miley Cyrus could fit into. His hair is gelled to the side and I can see he's shaved the one side of his head almost down to the bone.

"Yeah, well, you look... okay. Better than yesterday anyways."

"And you look like you fell headfirsht into a lawnmower."

"Still an asshole, I see."

"Hm sowy," I tell him, sighing through my teeth.

"Dad, I always thought you were one step away from joining the KKK, honestly, I pretty much thought you were Hitler."

217

"Yeah, well, I kind of gathered that."

"But I see it now, I do. And you're not that. You're just a lonely old man trying to figure shit out, and I get it. I really do. Because it's like I've been trying to tell you, our society is fucked. There's a precedence put on the wrong things, people focus on the wrong things. Maybe you can agree with me on that now, or maybe not, but either way, I'm proud of you dad. I really am."

I nod my head, trying to think of something poignant to say.

"How'sh Alisha?"

"Oh, she's good. She's going to try and come up this weekend..."

"That'sh good."

"She fights with me, you know? Like you do."

"Like me?"

"Yeah," he says, and I can see that it pains him by the way he grits his teeth. "She tells me I don't realize how good I have it. How lucky we are."

"Ha!" I half laugh, half yelp, looking down at myself lying half dead in this stiff hospital bed. "Yesh, we truly are the lucky one-sh!"

Thomas frowns, looking away out towards the hospital hallway.

"Hey," I say, reaching out to him with my good hand. "We are, though. We are lucky."

"Thanks dad," he says, taking my hand and squeezing it for a brief moment before letting go. "You know, I always knew you weren't a complete asshole."

"Thank you, shun."

"But, I always knew you were fucking crazy as well," he adds with a grin. "I can't believe you actually burned our fucking house down. That was next level, man."

"Yeah, well, ush old-timersh do things all the way. We don't shtop half-way, unlike you little shit-sh."

"Yeah, yeah," he says, pausing then to sigh. "Dad, why did you think I was gay?"

"Oh, I don't know, Tom. Probably becaush I never knew you that well..."

He sighs then, looking at me with his hazel eyes that I've never

218

really noticed until this instance. "You know, I always did want to make you proud. And the problem was, the more I saw that you weren't... like with the hockey and all... I guess it just made me resent you all the more, and so I guess that's when I started consciously trying to do everything opposite from how you would have..."

"It'sh okay," I tell him, not bothering to point out just how similar we were in that way. If only my son could have met the nineteen-year-old Markus. It would probably ruin his life to realize that we were essentially the same person, except I never wore pants that tight.

"What about you and mom?"

"We're getting divor-shed."

He looks at me in disbelief, and I can see the anger rising in his chest, but I cut in before he can say anything.

"We're not giving up though, shon. Giving up would be for your mother and I to shtay together. We aren't meant for each other, Tom. It'sh just the way it ish. You can't ex-sh-plain it, that'sh what I'fe learned. Don't efen attempt to try to ex-sh-plain love."

"I just want you both to be happy," he replies.

"Never change, shun."

"Thanks dad," he says. "Oh, and I snuck you in a little something..."

Thomas produces a mini mickey of Forty Creek Whiskey from his back pocket, depositing it beneath my pillow. My face aches but I cannot erase the smile which is causing the pain.

"Don't let the nurse find it, she looks like a proper see you next Tuesday."

And with that, my son exits my room, saying good-bye and telling me he will be back tomorrow, and as I watch him leave, there is a ringing in my ears and a quickened pace to my swollen heart as I realize that I've just had a legitimately meaningful moment with my son. After nineteen fucking year, all it took was a broken jaw and a few broken ribs to finally connect with the boy that I created. Seems fair, I guess, given the circumstances.

I hit the morphine button, but the usual tidal wave of euphoria

219

does not come. I hit it again and again, but to no avail. Just then the nurse pokes her pit-bullish head into the room, watching me for a moment before saying;

"We cut off your morphine supply, Mr. Stanfield. We were starting to worry that you were abusing the substance, so, you will just have to try and deal with the pain as best you can. I can bring you a couple Tylenol if you like."

"No tank-sh," I sigh.

Thomas was always a very perceptive boy, and I smile again to myself as I feel pride swell inside my chest. A perceptive, politically active, foul-mouthed man. Maybe I wasn't the worst parent after all...

I awake from my pain induced slumber to find a giant Dick sitting beside my bed.

"Hi Dick."

"Hey, you're finally up. I've been here for almost an hour."

"Sho shorry to inconvenien-sh you."

"Oh no inconvenience here, I'm enjoying my extended lunch break."

"I'm shure you are."

"Mark, you okay?"

"Yeah, yeah," I sigh. "Thank-sh for sh-topping by."

"Of course man, what the hell happened?"

"Well, I guesh I tried to be a good guy for one-sh."

"That's what you get," Dick says smiling.

"Yeah, I know."

"Did you get a couple shots in at least?"

"Nah, come on, man. Look at me. Even if I did pun-sh the guy I probably would have broken my damn hand."

"Well, I'm glad you're okay."

"Yeah, thank-sh."

We sit there in silence for a while, Dick twiddling his thumbs together and staring at the floor, and as much as I appreciate him being here, I can't ignore the fact that he seems to be having trouble making eye contact with me.

"You made the news," he says.

"Oh yeah?"

"Front page on the Metro."

"Finally, a little goddamn recognishion."

Dick forces a chuckle.

"You've had yourself quite a week."

"Yeah... it'sh been, shomething."

"Yeah," Dick nods.

"We going to go for shome lunch beer-sh when I get out of here, or what?"

"Ah I don't know, Mark," he sighs. "I'm not sure it'd be good for me to be down at the Lion's Cock drinking with the fella who burned his house down and was found half-beaten to death in a pool of booze and cocaine."

I laugh because I sincerely think he's joking, but when I realize he's not, my laughter stops.

"Are you sh-erious right now?"

"Come on, Mark. You know I'm thinking about running next election, and there's certain expectations, you know. We can still hang out or whatever..."

"Un-fucking-believable."

"Mark..."

"No, save it, Dick," I say.

Dick stares at me stunned, his mouth hanging open. "I'm still your friend, Mark..."

"What good ish a friend who can't have lunch beer-sh?"

"Mark, come on."

"Fuck off."

He stammers a bit and then leaves. I almost feel bad before I realize what a selfish prick he is, and then I pass out again.

That night I'm lying in bed and my ass is asleep but it hurts too much to move. Part of me wishes I was in Intensive Care because then at least I'd have a TV in my room and wouldn't be lift to writhe and twist with the thoughts in my head, wrestling with them like a stalker in the darkness, they continuously swarm around me, poking and prodding at me with their pointed fingers; you have no one left; you are all alone; you're life hasn't

221

amounted to a single goddamn thing; and, most distressingly; you deserve all of this.

I sigh audibly, bringing a hand up to my face and gently brushing my jaw. The swelling seemed to be down, and I can finally open my left eye fully again. The door to my room sits ajar and I take faint notice of the clock that reads 1:32am. Despite the time, the hallways are still alive with stuttered movement, carts being wheeled by and soft whispers of nurses and doctors, undoubtedly conspiring to murder me. All we have to do is wait till the poor bastard falls asleep, and it's as simple as a pillow and a little bit of pressure. You see the gut on that guy? Not a chance he'll put up a fight.

I can hear muffled steps shuffling down the hallway, and when they stop outside my door I can feel the hairs on my neck begin to stand up, picturing the silhouette of my dead daughter standing out in the hallway, her pale skin glowing in the darkness. My door creeks open wider and much to my horror, I see her. Standing in the doorway with her hair masking her face, and I can only imagine that she is here to finish me off. To repay the favour I so generously bestowed upon her.

I moan as she takes a step into the room, her footfalls causing me to feel all hollow and deflated.

"Pl-l-l-eash..." I stammer, clutching the bed sheets with clenched fists.

"Markus?"

"Cheryl?"

"Hi," she says, coming into focus as she moves beside my bed, her hospital gown draped over her slender body. Her hair is done up in a lazy pony-tail, and her face is gaunt and pale, deep bags burrowed beneath her eyes. I had never really seen her without make-up on. She looked about twenty years older, poor girl.

God, you're an asshole. You realize she just tried to kill herself, right?

Oh, shit. Right.

Our eyes remain locked for a few silent seconds, and in my head I can hear a cold wind blowing between my ears, my face turning red, and even though I want to scream at her, berate and degrade her... I just don't have the maliciousness left in me, all of my hatred and scorn left staining the floor of Jim's apartment in warm red pools.

"I saw your story in the Metro," she says, biting her lip. "Typical that they stuck us both in the same hospital, eh?"

"Sheem-sh to be our luck."

"I'm sorry," she says.

"Me too."

"I went by your house the day it burned down."

There's been reports of a young girl sighted in the area...

"I went there to find you, to yell at you... but, I saw you dancing in the window with this crazy smile on your face... and I'm not going to lie, it broke my heart. You looked genuinely happy."

"That washn't happineesh, that wash inshanity."

"Was that my fault?" she asks.

"No," I shake my head, my jaw making a funny clicking sound. "Did you get my letter?"

"Yesh."

She sighs then, looking around the room as if there might be some sort of device or person who might be able to help eradicate the thick fog of awkward air that is currently swirling all around us.

"Spencer hasn't even been here to visit me yet... he sent me a text message saying it would raise too many questions..."

"You need to leaf him," I mumble, my jaw aching. My tongue feels like it weighs about ten pounds.

"I know," she says, sighing again. "What about you and your wife?"

"Oh, you know... I'd rather not talk about it."

"Okay," she says, frowning and staring at the goddamn floor again. So many fleeting thoughts swarming amongst the craters and crevices of my mind.

"Cheryl... are you okay?" I ask her, reaching out with my hand, despite the throbbing pain in my side.

"Yes," she says, taking my hand in hers. "I'm better than I was."

"Good, I'm glad."

And I feel her hand squeezing and so I squeeze right back and she smiles down at me as a nurse shuffles by in the hallway.

"When are they letting you out of here?" she asks.

"Tomorrow."

"I'm getting out today," she says, peering past me and out the small square window. "It's been decided that I no longer pose a threat to myself or others..."

"Well... that'sh, good?"

"What do they know?" she scuffs. "What does anybody really know?"

"I know that you desherve better."

And she looks at me then, her eyes all glistening and face tied up in a tight little knot, and she leans down and gives me a hug that cracks my neck and causes a fresh wave of pain to explode in the left side of my jaw, but it's not so bad and I can feel her tears all hot and wet against my cheek. Why is it that everyone ends up crying when they visit me? I can't tell if that's a good thing or a bad thing... but one thing was for certain, I would have to tell her about the whole syphilis thing at some other point, because to spoil this little moment with such toxic news would be just downright criminal...

She finally lets go and moves to leave the room, but stopping at the door, she turns back, her hand upon the inside of the door frame, and she looks quite good, to be honest, with her legs exposed and all, and she looks at me one last time and says; "Oh by the way, you may want to ask the doctor for a blood test. Apparently, I have syphilis."

Gee, thanks Cheryl. Doesn't anyone have a shred of sentimentality left... oh shit... never mind.

I am a hypocrite.

My father is coming to pick me up today, and I cannot wait to escape this all white room with the teal coloured bed sheets that smell of chlorine and leave my skin feeling dry and itchy. I've lost track of what day it is, which suits me just fine. My jaw aches but the pain in my ribs has subsided a bit.

The surly nurse comes in to find me sitting upright in my bed with my balls hanging out from my hospital gown. I watch her study them briefly with a disgusted look upon her face, as if she were looking down the barrel of a birthing process in its crowning stage.

"Mr. Stanfield, I will remind you that patients being discharged are required to be out of their rooms by noon," and I watch her eyes snap over towards the round clock on the wall which read 12:17.

"Yesh, yesh, I hear you," I say, pushing myself from the bed and standing with considerable effort. "Thank you for being sh-uch a treat this pash week," I tell her, a sharp pain shooting up the side of my face.

She scoffs and shuffles out of the room without another word.

And who said there was anything wrong with the Canadian Healthcare System? At least I didn't need surgery. Lord knows how long the wait would be.

My legs are shaky as I make my way over towards the plastic chair where a pile of my clothes are sitting their neatly folded (I assume Trace is to thank for this). I take faint notice that they are different from the blood-stained clothes in which I came here wearing, and I wonder where those blood-stained clothes go after being peeled from the patient? Probably some sort of furnace or incinerator.

I hear the sound of more shuffling steps approaching my doorway as I struggle to pull on my pants, pain shooting up my side with every inch I bend over. Pay close attention people, this is what you get for trying to be a good guy.

I prepare myself for another passive aggressive onslaught from Miss Nurse Lady.

"Markus."

I turn to find Jim standing in the doorway, his face a collage of bandages and stitches. He takes a step further into the room and stops, looking much like a nervous dog who knows he just committed some sort of indecent act. His face is a mass of purple and yellow bruises, and I see is missing both of his front teeth.

225

"Hello Jim."

"I... well... I wanted to stop by before you left. I'm glad I caught you," he sounds all clogged up on account of his busted nose, like he's just come down with a serious case of the flu. I can only imagine just how mangled it was, considering he most definitely had a deviated septum thanks to the copious amounts of cocaine he had snorted over the years.

I stare back at him from the corner of the room, my pants halfway up my legs, unsure as to what I should say.

"I just wanted to say thank-you."

"No problem," I shrug.

And at this point he turns and leaves. Too embarrassed with himself to bother with any grand gesture or fantastic speech. Too proud to promise never to behave in such a way again. And I can hear those same beeps echoing throughout the empty hospital hallways, the fluorescent lights reflecting bright off the linoleum floors, because this is real life, my friends, and there are no happy endings... only tepid resolutions, like cold coffee, sitting all stale upon your tongue.

Epilogue

I'm driving down Sussex to meet my son and A'ishah at the National Art Museum to check out the Da Vinci exhibit. The sun hangs high in the sky, casting a yellow glow upon the pavement. The streets are speckled with summer tourists, and I study them with their backpacks and cameras slung around their shoulders, walking hand in hand with their families, necks turning this way and that like a pack of pigeons.

The traffic is heavy on Sussex (typical) but for once I don't really mind because I got my jaw unwired yesterday and I can finally breathe through my mouth again (yes, I am a mouth breather, get over it). I roll down my window and suck in some of the summer air, hanging my arm out of the window and feeling like a teenager for the briefest of moments, I reach out and turn up the volume on the radio, unsure as to what song is currently playing on the Hot 89.9 (it sounds like robots having sex, to be frank), and not caring, only that it's music and the sun is out and I can move my mouth again, finally.

Ol' Dick reached out to me after the Mayor gave me honorary distinction for helping to save Jim's life. They only gave me the damn award because he was a veteran. I mean, if he had happened to be just another alcoholic drug-addict, no one would have given a shit, and I guess that's maybe the problem right there. Anyways, I'm still going to meetings and so is Jim, and I guess that's good. He doesn't talk as much anymore, but from what I can tell the bastard is staying sober, which is really all that matters.

Oh, and I told Dick to fuck off.

I pass by the eighteen-million-dollar spider that stands out front of the Art Gallery along Sussex, it's long black legs spindling down, casting skinny shadows upon the white paved sidewalks.

And passing by this overpriced piece of metal would usually flare up feelings of disgust and annoyance in me, except not today, because the insurance company couldn't prove that I burned my house down (despite the fact that pretty much everyone knows I did), and so we received our settlement, which I of course was forced to split with Trace on account of the divorce, which suited me just fine considering she was forced to split her publishing bonus with me (and my friends chastised me for not signing a pre-nub!). Tracy is now a best-selling Canadian author, and Love has no Language can be found in all your local Shoppers Drug Marts and Independent Grocers throughout the country.

It's not millions, but it certainly is enough for me to pay off my debts and live comfortably.

I sold what was left of our property and closed my real estate office.

For the first time in a long time, I feel free. I feel like maybe, just maybe, there was still some enjoyment to be cajoled from this life.

My phone buzzes and I see a text from my son that reads; dad, where are you? You're late.

Yeah, yeah, not too much enjoyment. I get it.

Across the street I can see her as I sit waiting at the red light. She's wearing an all-white dress which frills out at the waist, her somewhat pale arms exposed from the shoulder down to her bosom, and she's got full red lips and wide eyes that can probably see in all directions at once. She looked lovely, to be honest. I smile at her and she smiles back with a full set of pearly white teeth, her long brunette hair cascading down her shoulders in elegant curls.

I find myself a parking spot along York Street (hallelujah!), and stepping out of my car, I take another deep breath, letting the delicious air fill my mouth and lungs, closing my eyes and opening them again, I peer up into the beautiful summer sky, and I can't deny, it certainly does look like a beautiful day to go canoeing...

Printed in Great Britain
by Amazon

56182854R00135